Lamb

BLOOMSBURY KITCHEN LIBRARY

Lamb

Bloomsbury Books
London

This edition published 1995 by Bloomsbury Books,
an imprint of The Godfrey Cave Group,
42 Bloomsbury Street, London, WC1B 3QJ.

ISBN 1 85471 572 0

Printed and bound in Great Britain.

Contents

Medallions with Watercress Sauce

Serves 4

Working time:
about 35
minutes

Total time:
about 45
minutes

Calories
200
Protein
25g
Cholesterol
90mg
Total fat
11g
Saturated fat
5g
Sodium
90mg

1 kg	loin of lamb, boned, trimmed, eye cut diagonally into 12 slices, fillet reserved for another use	**2¼ lb**
30 cl	unsalted brown or chicken stock	**½ pint**
2	bunches watercress, washed	**2**
4	sage leaves, or ⅛ tsp dried sage	**4**

½ tsp	salt	**½ tsp**
	white pepper	
1 tbsp	apple jelly	**1 tbsp**
1 tbsp	Worcester sauce, mixed with 1 tbsp water	**1 tbsp**
1 tbsp	fromage frais	**1 tbsp**

To make the watercress sauce, boil the stock until the liquid is reduced by half—5 to 10 minutes. Strip the leaves from the watercress, reserving four sprigs for garnish, and add the watercress and sage leaves to the reduced boiling stock. Cook the stock for a further 1 minute, allow it to cool slightly, then purée it in a blender or food processor. Transfer it to a small pan, season with half of the salt and some pepper and add the apple jelly. Stir the sauce over low heat until the jelly has melted, then remove the pan from the heat.

Season the lamb slices with the remaining ¼ teaspoon of salt and some pepper. Lightly brush a large non-stick frying pan with oil and brown six of the slices over high heat for 1 minute on each side. Reduce the heat to medium, add half of the Worcester sauce mixture and cook for a further 30 seconds to 1 minute on each side for rare to medium meat. Transfer the meat to a platter and keep it warm. Cook the remaining slices in the same way.

Heat the watercress sauce through, then remove it from the heat and stir in the fromage frais. Serve the lamb with the sauce, garnished with the reserved sprigs of watercress.

Flambéed Cutlets with Stuffed Apricots

Serves 4

Working time about 40 minutes

Total time: about 7 hours (includes marinating)

Calories 260
Protein 31g
Cholesterol 75mg
Total fat 8g
Saturated fat 4g
Sodium 175mg

8	best end of neck cutlets (about 90 g/3 oz each), trimmed of fat	8
2 tbsp	coarsely chopped fresh ginger root	2 tbsp
2	garlic cloves, coarsely chopped	2
1	small onion, coarsely chopped	1
15 cl	fresh orange juice	¼ pint
¼ tsp	virgin olive oil	¼ tsp
125 g	mushrooms, finely chopped	4 oz
¼ tsp	salt	¼ tsp
	freshly ground black pepper	
8	dried whole apricots, soaked in water for 6 hours, or overnight	8
2 tbsp	brandy	2 tbsp
	parsley, for garnish (optional)	

Lay the cutlets in a shallow dish or casserole. Blend together the ginger, garlic, half the chopped onion and the orange juice in a food processor. Spoon the purée over the cutlets, cover and leave to marinate for at least 6 hours, or overnight, turning them once.

Heat the oil in a heavy frying pan. Add the mushrooms and the remaining onion, season them with half the salt and some pepper and sauté over medium heat until they are soft.

Dry the apricots on paper towels and fill them with the mushroom and onion stuffing.

Remove the cutlets from the marinade and pat them dry, strain the marinade and reserve

it. Preheat a non-stick sauté pan and sear the cutlets for 1 minute on each side. Add the brandy and light it with a taper. When the flame dies down, arrange the stuffed apricots in the pan, pour in half of the marinade and sprinkle with the remaining salt. Cover and cook over low heat until the juices are still slightly pink—about 10 minutes.

Arrange the meat and stuffed apricots on a warm platter. Skim off any fat from the juices in the pan, then add the remaining marinade, bring it to the boil and simmer for 1 minute. Spoon the sauce over the lamb and serve, garnished with parsley.

Lamb Medallions on Courgette Pancakes

Serves 4

Working (and total) time: about 30 minutes

Calories 235
Protein 26g
Cholesterol 70mg
Total fat 9g
Saturated fat 4g
Sodium 295mg

1 kg	loin, boned and trimmed of fat, eye only	**2¼ lb**
3 tbsp	cut chives or finely chopped spring onions, for garnish	**3 tbsp**
	Courgette pancakes	
350 g	courgettes grated	**12 oz**
1	carrot, grated	**1**

1	egg white	**1**
3 tbsp	freshly grated Parmesan cheese	**3 tbsp**
2 tbsp	wholemeal flour	**2 tbsp**
2	garlic cloves, finely chopped	**. 2**
¼ tsp	salt	**¼ tsp**
	freshly ground black pepper	
1 tsp	safflower oil	**1 tsp**

Cut the eye of into eight slices. With a meat bat or the flat of a heavy knife pound each slice between plastic film or greaseproof paper to a thickness of about 5 mm (¼ inch). Set the medallions aside.

Combine all the pancake ingredients except the oil in a bowl and mix them well.

Heat a large, non-stick frying pan over medium heat. Add the oil and spread it over the bottom with a paper towel. Drop four 2 tablespoon mounds of the pancake mixture into the pan, allowing ample room between them. With a spatula, spread out each mound to form a pancake about 7.5 cm (3 inches) in diameter. Cook the pancakes until they are lightly browned—about 3 minutes on each side. Transfer the pancakes to a baking sheet and keep them warm in a very low oven. Cook four more pancakes in the same way.

Increase the heat under the pan to high. Add the medallions to the pan and cook them until they are browned about 2 minutes oil each side. -

Put two courgette pancakes on each of four plates; top each pancake with a lamb medallion. Sprinkle the medallions with the cut chives or chopped spring onions, and serve at once.

Loin and Liver Cassis

Serves 4

Working time:
about 30
minutes

Total time:
about 40
minutes

Calories
175
Protein
18g
Cholesterol
105mg
Total fat
8g
Saturated fat
3g
Sodium
35mg

300 g	lean lamb trimmed, thinly sliced and flattened	**10 oz**
60 g	lamb's liver, very thinly sliced	**2 oz**
12	shallots	**12**
7 g	unsalted butter	**¼oz**
2 tbsp	plus 1 tsp crème de cassis	**2 tbsp**

1¼tsp	blackcurrant or red wine vinegar	**1¼tsp**
¾tsp	salt	**¾tsp**
15 cl	unsalted chicken stock	**¼ pint**
2 tsp	plain flour	**2 tsp**
	freshly ground black pepper	

Place the shallots in a small, heavy saucepan with the butter, the teaspoon of créme de cassis, ½ teaspoon of the vinegar, ¼ teaspoon of the salt and 3 tablespoons of water. Cover tightly, bring to the boil and simmer until the shallots are tender—about 25 minutes. Remove the lid, and boil off the residual liquid to glaze the shallots, shaking the pan occasionally. Set aside and keep warm.

Meanwhile, pour the stock and the remaining créme de cassis into a separate saucepan. Boil it rapidly until the liquid has reduced by half—5 to 10 minutes. Set aside.

Sift the flour with some pepper and toss the liver in the seasoned flour until it is evenly coated. Brush a large, heavy frying pan lightly with oil, place it over very high heat and sear the slices of loin for 20 to 30 seconds on each side. Transfer them to a heated serving dish, sprinkle them with pepper and keep them warm. Reduce the heat to low, brush the pan with a little more oil and cook the floured slices of liver for 20 to 30 seconds, stirring constantly. Remove the liver and set it aside.

Increase the heat under the pan and add the remaining teaspoon of vinegar. Allow it to bubble for a few seconds, then add the reduced stock and the remaining ½ teaspoon of salt. Bring to the boil, return the liver to the pan and simmer for a further 30 seconds before spooning the sauce and liver over the slices of loin. Serve with the glazed shallots.

Kasha-Coated Lamb with Parsley-Garlic Sauce

Serves 4

Working (and total) time: about 20 minutes

Calories
410
Protein
35g
Cholesterol
85mg
Total fat
14g
Saturated fat
5g
Sodium
75mg

4	lamb slices (about 125 g/4 oz each), cut from the fillet end of the leg, trimmed and flattened	**4**
1	egg white	**1**
1 tbsp	fresh lemon juice	**1 tbsp**
200 g	toasted buckwheat groats (kasha)	**7 oz**
¼ tsp	salt	**¼ tsp**
	freshly ground black pepper	
1 tbsp	virgin olive oil	**1 tbsp**
½ tbsp	unsalted butter	**½ tbsp**
1	shallot, finely chopped	**1**
1	garlic clove, finely chopped	**1**
60 g	parsley, chopped	**2 oz**
1	large ripe tomato, skinned, seeded and puréed	**1**

In a shallow bowl, whisk together the egg white and lemon juice. Spread the buckwheat groats on a plate. Sprinkle the lamb slices with the salt and some pepper. Dip a slice in the egg white mixture, then dredge it in the buckwheat groats, coating both sides. Repeat the process to coat the remaining slices.

Heat the oil and butter in a large, heavy or non-stick frying pan over high heat. Add the coated lamb slices and cook them until they are lightly browned on one side—about 3 minutes. Turn the slices and cook them for 2 minutes more to brown the second side. Transfer the slices to a warmed platter.

Add the chopped shallot, garlic and parsley to the pan and cook them for 1 minute. Stir in the puréed tomato and a generous grinding of black pepper. Cook the mixture for 1 minute more, then pour it over the lamb slices. Serve immediately.

Lamb with Aubergine and Parmesan

Serves 4

Working
time: about
40 minutes

Total time:
about 1 hour

Calories
450
Protein
34g
Cholesterol
80mg
Total fat
10g
Saturated fat
4g
Sodium
235mg

500 g	lean lamb (from the leg or loin), trimmed and cut into pieces	**1 lb**
250 g	pasta shells	**8 oz**
1 tsp	virgin olive oil	**1 tsp**
250 g	pearl onions, blanched in boiling water for 2 minutes and peeled	**8 oz**

250 g	small mushrooms wiped clean	**8 oz**
350 g	aubergine, cut into cubes	**12 oz**
1 tsp	fresh thyme, or ½ tsp dried thyme freshly ground black pepper	**1 tsp**
15 g	Parmesan cheese, shaved with a vegetable peeler or grated	**½ oz**

Add the pasta to 3 litres (5 pints) of boiling water with 1½ teaspoons of salt. Start testing the pasta after 6 minutes and cook it until it is *al dente*. Drain, then rinse the pasta to prevent the shells from sticking together. Set aside while you cook the meat and vegetables.

Heat a large, non-stick sauté pan over high heat. Add the pieces of lamb and sauté them until they are browned on all sides—about 3 minutes. Reduce the heat to medium and cook the lamb for 3 minutes more. Remove the meat from the pan and set it aside.

Add the olive oil and onions to the sauté pan. Cover the pan and cook the onions, stirring, until they are browned—about 15 minutes. Add the mushrooms and aubergine cubes, then increase the heat to high, and sauté the vegetables until all of them are browned and the mushrooms and aubergine are soft—6 to 8 minutes.

Return the lamb to the pan; add the pasta, the thyme and a generous grinding of pepper. Sauté the mixture until the pasta is heated through—about 3 minutes. Spoon the mixture into a warmed serving dish and top it with the cheese. Serve immediately.

Stir-Fried Vegetables with Shredded Lamb

Serves 4

Working
(and total)
time: about
40 minutes

Calories
255
Protein
21g
Cholesterol
50mg
Total fat
13g
Saturated fat
3g
Sodium
265mg

350 g	lean lamb (from the loin), cut into thin strips	**12 oz**	**1**	onion, peeled and sliced	**1**
4 tbsp	sake or dry sherry	**4 tbsp**	**175 g**	baby sweetcorn, halved lengthwise if large	**6 oz**
2 tbsp	soy sauce or shoyu	**2 tbsp**	**1**	sweet red pepper, seeded, chopped	**1**
1 tsp	cornflour	**1 tsp**	**175 g**	cucumber, halved lengthwise, seeded and sliced	**6 oz**
2 tbsp	safflower oil	**2 tbsp**	**175 g**	small mange-tout, stems and strings removed	**6 oz**
1 tbsp	finely chopped fresh ginger root	**1 tbsp**			

Mix together the sake, soy sauce and cornflour in a small bowl and set the mixture aside.

Heat the oil in a wok or large, heavy sauté pan until it is hot but not smoking. Add the chopped ginger and onion slices, and stir-fry for 1 minute over high heat, then add the baby sweetcorn and continue to stir-fry for 1 more minute.

Add the strips of lamb a few at a time, stirring constantly until they are completely sealed and lightly coloured, then add the pepper and cucumber and stir-fry for a further minute.

Lastly, add the mange-tout and stir-fry for 1 minute. Pour the sake mixture over the meat and vegetables in the wok and bring it to the boil, stirring until the liquid thickens. Serve immediately.

Loin and Liver in Yellow Bean Sauce

Serves 4

Working time:
about 20
minutes

Total time:
about 30
minutes

Calories
235
Protein
22g
Cholesterol
265mg
Total fat
13g
Saturated fat
3g
Sodium
425mg

175 g	lean lamb (from the loin), trimmed and cut into thin strips	**6 oz**
175 g	lamb's liver, cut into thin strips	**6 oz**
2 tsp	light low-sodium soy sauce	**2 tsp**
2 tsp	Chinese rice wine or dry sherry	**2 tsp**
1 tsp	sesame oil	**1 tsp**
1½ tsp	cornflour	**1½ tsp**
200 g	spring onions	**7 oz**
2 cm	piece fresh ginger root	**¾ inch**
1	garlic clove	**1**

2 tsp	safflower oil	**2 tsp**
½	fresh red chili pepper, seeded and thinly sliced	**½**
	nori seaweed, shredded, for garnish	
	Yellow bean sauce	
3 tbsp	yellow bean sauce	**3 tbsp**
½ tsp	sugar	**½ tsp**
1 tsp	dark low-sodium soy sauce or shoyu	**1 tsp**
2 tsp	Chinese rice wine or dry sherry	**2 tsp**

Put the loin and liver strips into separate bowls. Mix together the light soy sauce, rice wine, sesame oil and cornflour and divide this between the two bowls. Coat the meat and leave to marinate for 15 minutes. Mix the ingredients for the yellow bean sauce and set aside.

Cut the spring onions into 6 cm (2½ inch) lengths. Cut the white sections in half lengthwise; keep the white and the green parts separate. Bruise the ginger and garlic with the side of a heavy knife.

Gently heat a wok and add the safflower oil. Add the ginger and garlic and cook until they turn light brown. Rub the garlic and ginger all round the wok, then discard them. Increase the heat and stir-fry the loin, followed by the liver, the white parts of the spring onions and the yellow bean sauce. Toss each ingredient for about 15 seconds before adding the next: Add the chili and stir-fry for another 10 seconds, then stir in the green parts of the spring onions.

Serve immediately, with garnish.

Warm Herbed Salad

Serves 4

Working time: about 30 minutes

Total time: about 3 hours and 30 minutes (includes marinating)

Calories 260
Protein 31g
Cholesterol 90mg
Total fat 14g
Saturated fat 6g
Sodium 380mg

4	lamb slices (about 125 g/4 oz each), cut from the fillet end of the leg, trimmed and flattened	**4**
12.5 cl	dry white wine	**4 fl oz**
1 tbsp	chopped fresh tarragon	**1 tbsp**
4 tsp	chopped fresh dill	**4 tsp**
4 tsp	chopped fresh chervil	**4 tsp**
1 tbsp	safflower oil	**1 tbsp**
¾ tsp	salt	**¾ tsp**
	freshly ground black pepper	
100 g	cucumber, cut into bâtonnets	**3½ oz**
200 g	Batavian endive, washed, dried, trimmed and shredded	**7 oz**
2 tbsp	crème fraîche	**2 tbsp**
3 tbsp	thick Greek yogurt	**3 tbsp**
¼ tsp	sugar	**¼ tsp**

Cut each slice of meat into five strips. Place in a shallow dish with the wine, the tarragon and 3 teaspoons each of the dill and chervil. Marinate for 3 to 4 hours, turning half way through.

Remove the meat from the marinade and dry it well; reserve the marinade. Heat the oil in a wide, heavy frying pan until it is very hot but not smoking. Brown the meat for 30 seconds on each side, then remove it from the pan and season it with ½ teaspoon of the salt and some black pepper. Keep it warm.

Skim off any fat from the pan juices, then add the cucumber bâtonnets and cook gently over medium heat until they begin to soften—about 1½ minutes. Transfer them to a large bowl and add the endive.

Strain the reserved marinade into the frying pan and boil it over high heat until only 3 tablespoons of liquid remain. Remove the pan from the heat, stir in the crème fraîche and cook over low heat for 1 minute. Again remove the pan from the heat, and stir in the yogurt, the sugar and the remaining dill, chervil and salt. Pour the warm dressing over the endive and cucumber in the bowl and toss the salad. Place the strips of lamb on top and serve immediately.

Lamb Stroganoff

Serves 4

Working
(and total)
time: about
25 minutes

Calories
230
Protein
29g
Cholesterol
80mg
Total fat
12g
Saturated fat
5g
Sodium
175mg

500 g	lean lamb, trimmed and cut into thin strips	**1 lb**		**1 tsp**	Dijon mustard	**1 tsp**
1 tbsp	virgin olive oil	**1 tbsp**		**¼ tsp**	salt	**¼ tsp**
1	onion, finely chopped	**1**			freshly ground black pepper	
250 g	mushrooms, thinly sliced	**8 oz**		**1 tbsp**	chopped parsley	**1 tbsp**
4 tbsp	thick Greek yogurt	**4 tbsp**		**1 tbsp**	finely cut chives	**1 tbsp**

Heat the oil in a large, heavy frying pan over medium heat. Add the onion and cook it gently until soft but not brown—6 to 8 minutes. Transfer the onion to a plate. Add half of the lamb strips to the frying pan and cook them over high heat until they are lightly browned—1 to 2 minutes—then transfer them to the plate with the onion. Brown the remaining lamb strips, then return the first batch and the onion to the pan.

Add the mushrooms and cook over medium heat until they soften—4 to 5 minutes. Away from the heat, stir the yogurt and mustard into the mixture, then heat it through gently for 3 to 4 minutes. Season with the salt and some black pepper.

Transfer the stroganoff to a serving dish. Sprinkle it with the parsley and chives and serve immediately.

Lamb and Barley Salad

Serves 4

Working time:
about 20
minutes

Total time:
about 2 hours
(includes
chilling)

Calories
265
Protein
21g
Cholesterol
50mg
Total fat
10g
Saturated fat
4g
Sodium
275mg

350 g	lean lamb, trimmed and cut into cubes	**12 oz**
100 g	pearl barley	**3½ oz**
1½ tbsp	chopped fresh oregano, or ½ tsp dried oregano	**1½ tbsp**
1½ tbsp	virgin olive oil	**1½ tbsp**
¼ tsp	salt	**¼ tsp**

	freshly ground black pepper	
3 tbsp	red wine vinegar	**3 tbsp**
1	large ripe tomato, seeded and chopped	**1**
1	stick celery, chopped	**1**
90 g	red onion, chopped	**3 oz**
	lettuce leaves, for garnish	

Put the barley, half of the oregano and ¾ litre (1¼ pints) of water into 2 saucepan. Bring the water to the boil, then reduce the heat to maintain a steady simmer. Cover the pan and cook the barley until it is tender—about 50 minutes. Drain the barley, transfer it to a bowl, and stir in 1 tablespoon of the oil.

Heat the remaining oil in a heavy frying pan set over high heat. Add the lamb cubes and sprinkle them with the salt and some freshly ground pepper. Sauté the cubes,

stirring frequently, until they are lightly browned—about 2 minutes. Pour in the vinegar and cook for 30 seconds longer.

Transfer the contents of the pan to the bowl with the barley. Add the tomato, celery, onion, the remaining oregano and a generous grinding of pepper. Toss the salad well and chill it for at least 1 hour.

Just before serving, arrange the lettuce leaves on a plate or platter and mound the salad on top.

Marinated Cutlets with Caper and Parsley Sauce

Serves 6

Working time:
about 30
minutes

Total time:
about 2 hours
and 30 minutes
(includes
marinating)

Calories
255
Protein
27g
Cholesterol
85mg
Total fat
15g
Saturated fat
3g
Sodium
170mg

12	best end of neck cutlets (about 90 g/3 oz each), trimmed	12
1 tsp	virgin olive oil	1 tsp
1	garlic clove, finely chopped	1
1 tbsp	chopped parsley	1 tbsp
1 tsp	chopped fresh marjoram, or ¼tsp dried marjoram	1 tsp
1 tsp	chopped fresh thyme, or ¼tsp dried thyme	1 tsp
¼ tsp	salt	¼ tsp

½ tsp	freshly ground black pepper	½ tsp
	Caper and parsley sauce	
1 tsp	cornflour	1 tsp
8 cl	skimmed milk	3 fl oz
75 g	crème fraîche	2½ oz
4	pickled onions, chopped	4
2 tbsp	chopped parsley	2 tbsp
1 tbsp	finely chopped capers	1 tbsp
	freshly ground black pepper	

Using a sharp knife, scrape the ends of the rib bones free of any flesh or skin. Place the cutlets in a large shallow dish. Combine the olive oil, garlic, parsley, marjoram, thyme, salt and freshly ground pepper, and brush this mixture over both sides of the cutlets. Cover the dish and leave the cutlets to marinate in the refrigerator for 2 to 4 hours.

Preheat the grill to high while you make the sauce. Mix the cornflour with 1 tablespoon of the milk. Bring the remaining milk nearly to the boil in a small saucepan, add the cornflour paste and cook over low heat, stirring, until the milk thickens—2 to 3 minutes. Stir in the crème fraîche, pickled onions, parsley, capers and some pepper. Heat the sauce through, remove it from the heat and keep it warm while cooking the cutlets.

Cook the cutlets for 3 to 4 minutes on each side for rare to medium meat and serve them with the sauce.

Cutlets with Pernod

Serves 4

Working time:
about 25
minutes

Total time:
about 2 hours
and 30 minutes
(includes
marinating)

Calories
260
Protein
29g
Cholesterol
75mg
Total fat
13g
Saturated fat
6g
Sodium
280mg

8	best end of neck cutlets (about 90 g/3 oz each), trimmed	8
2	limes, finely grated rind and juice	2
4 tbsp	plain low-fat yogurt	4 tbsp
2	garlic cloves, crushed	2
2 tbsp	Pernod or other anise-flavoured spirit	2 tbsp
1 tbsp	chopped fresh thyme, or 1 tsp dried thyme	1 tbsp
1 tsp	muscovado sugar freshly ground black pepper	1 tsp
1 tsp	cornflour	1 tsp
$\frac{1}{2}$ tsp	salt	$\frac{1}{2}$ tsp
	lime wedges, for garnish	
	thyme sprigs, for garnish (optional)	

Put the lime rind and juice in a shallow dish with the yogurt, Pernod, thyme, crushed garlic, sugar and some freshly ground pepper. Whisk together with a fork, then place the lamb cutlets in the dish and turn them to coat them evenly. Cover the dish and leave the cutlets to marinate in the refrigerator for at least 2 hours, or preferably overnight.

Preheat the grill to high. Lift the cutlets out of the marinade, reserving the marinade, and

grill them for 3 to 4 minutes on each side for rare to medium meat.

While the cutlets are grilling, put the cornflour into a saucepan, blend in the marinade and add the salt. Bring the sauce to the boil and simmer for 3 minutes, stirring constantly. Arrange the cutlets on a warm serving dish and garnish with the lime wedges and thyme sprigs, if you are using them. Pass the sauce separately.

Noisettes with Julienned Vegetables

Serves 4

Working time: about 45 minutes

Total time: about 1 hour

Calories 265

Protein 38g

Cholesterol 100mg

Total fat 10g

Saturated fat 5g

Sodium 260mg

1	rack of lamb (about 1 kg/2¼lb), boned and trimmed	**1**
¼ tsp	salt	**¼ tsp**
	freshly ground black pepper	
1 tsp	finely chopped fresh oregano, or ¼ tsp dried oregano	**1 tsp**
2	large carrots, trimmed and julienned	**2**
3	sticks celery, trimmed and julienned	**3**
1	parsnip, peeled and julienned	**1**
2	leeks, trimmed, washed and julienned	**2**
1 tbsp	chopped parsley	**1 tbsp**

Season the boned side of the meat with the salt, a little pepper and the oregano. Roll the lamb into a cylinder, with the eye of the meat in the centre, and tie the roll at eight equally spaced intervals. Cut the roll into slices midway between each tie. Place the noisettes on the grill rack and set them aside.

Preheat the grill to high. Pour enough water into a saucepan to fill it 2.5 cm (1 inch) deep. Set a vegetable steamer in the pan and bring the water to the boil. Put the julienned carrots, celery and parsnip into the steamer, cover tightly, and steam for about 5 minutes; add the leeks and continue to steam for a further 3 minutes, until the vegetables are tender but still crisp.

Meanwhile, grill the noisettes for 3 to 5 minutes on each side for rare to medium meat. When the vegetables are cooked, toss them in the parsley.

Arrange the noisettes on a warm serving dish and surround them with the julienned vegetables.

Noisettes in a Fig Sauce

Serves 4

Working (and total) time: about 35 minutes

Calories 205
Protein 27g
Cholesterol 80mg
Total fat 7g
Saturated fat 3g
Sodium 270mg

8	loin chops (about 100 g/3½oz each) trimmed, boned and tied into noisettes	**8**
6	dried figs, finely chopped	**6**
2 tbsp	balsamic vinegar, or 1½ tbsp red wine vinegar mixed with ½ tsp honey	**2 tbsp**

2 tbsp	Madeira	**2 tbsp**
2 tsp	Worcester sauce	**2 tsp**
20 cl	unsalted chicken stock	**7 fl oz**
½ tsp	salt	**½ tsp**
	freshly ground black pepper	
4	fresh figs, sliced	**4**

Preheat the grill to high while you make the sauce. Put the dried figs, vinegar, Madeira and Worcester sauce in a small saucepan and simmer until the liquid reduces to a thick syrup—4 to 5 minutes. Add the chicken stock and bring the mixture to the boil; reduce the heat and simmer uncovered for 2 minutes. Remove the saucepan from the heat and press the mixture through a sieve to make a smooth sauce. Return the sauce to the pan and keep it warm, uncovered, over low heat while you cook the noisettes.

Season the noisettes with the salt and some freshly ground pepper and grill them for 2 to 4 minutes on each side for rare to medium meat. Serve immediately with the sauce and sliced fresh figs.

Noisettes with Glazed Potatoes and Gooseberry Purée

2	racks of lamb (about 600 g/1¼lb each), trimmed, boned, tied and cut into 12 noisettes	**2**	**400 g**	tiny new potatoes, scrubbed	**14 oz**
2 tsp	virgin olive oil	**2 tsp**		fresh chervil, for garnish	
	freshly ground black pepper			**Minted gooseberry purée**	
7 g	unsalted butter	**¼ oz**	**500 g**	fresh gooseberries, topped and tailed, or frozen gooseberries, thawed	**1 lb**
2	shallots, finely chopped	**2**	**2**	mint sprigs plus six leaves	**2**
15 cl	unsalted chicken stock	**¼ pint**	**1 tsp**	light brown sugar	**1 tsp**
⅛ tsp	salt	**⅛ tsp**	**¼ tsp**	salt	**¼ tsp**

Brush the noisettes with the olive oil and rub them all over with freshly ground pepper. Arrange them on a grill pan and set aside.

To make the purée, place the gooseberries in a heavy saucepan with the sprigs of mint, the sugar and 1 tablespoon of water. Cover and cook gently until the gooseberries are soft—15 to 30 minutes. Remove the mint sprigs and purée in a blender with the fresh mint leaves and the salt. Pass the purée through a nylon sieve; set aside and keep it warm.

Melt the butter in a heavy saucepan and gently cook the shallots, covered, until they are soft—about 5 minutes. Add the stock and salt, bring it to the boil, then add the potatoes and cook, partly-covered, until tender—20 to 25 minutes. Meanwhile, preheat the grill to high.

Remove the lid from the pan and boil the stock rapidly until no liquid remains and the potatoes are glossy—about 3 minutes. Shake the pan regularly during this process. Keep warm until ready to serve.

Grill the noisettes for 3 to 4 minutes on each side for rare to medium meat. Serve with the glazed potatoes and chervil garnish. Serve the purée separately.

Sweet and Spicy Grilled Lamb

Serves 4

Working time: about 1 hour

Total time: about 2 hours (includes marinating)

Calories 310
Protein 23g
Cholesterol 70mg
Total fat 8g
Saturated fat 3g
Sodium 205mg

1 kg	loin, boned and trimmed, eye only	2 lb
	freshly ground black pepper	
$\frac{1}{4}$ tsp	ground allspice	$\frac{1}{4}$ tsp
$\frac{1}{4}$ tsp	ground cloves	$\frac{1}{4}$ tsp
2 tbsp	fresh lemon juice	2 tbsp
2 tbsp	light brown sugar	2 tbsp

	Cherry ketchup	
225 g	sweet cherries, stoned	$7\frac{1}{2}$ oz
4 tbsp	light brown sugar	4 tbsp
$\frac{1}{4}$ tsp	salt	$\frac{1}{4}$ tsp
6 tbsp	cider vinegar	6 tbsp
7.5 cm	strip of lemon rind	3 inch
$\frac{1}{2}$ tsp	ground ginger	$\frac{1}{2}$ tsp
2	cinnamon sticks	2
$\frac{1}{8}$ tsp	cayenne pepper	$\frac{1}{8}$ tsp

To make the ketchup, combine the cherries, brown sugar, salt, vinegar, lemon rind, ginger, cinnamon sticks and cayenne pepper in a heavy-bottomed saucepan. Bring the mixture to a simmer and cook it until it has thickened—about 15 minutes. Discard the cinnamon sticks and pour the mixture into a food processor or blender. Purée the mixture, then strain it into a bowl and allow it to cool.

To prepare a marinade for the meat, mix a generous grinding of pepper with the allspice, cloves, lemon juice and brown sugar in a small bowl. Put the eye of loin in a

shallow dish and pour the marinade over it, rubbing the spices into the meat. Let the lamb marinate at room temperature for 1 hour, turning it every 15 minutes.

If you plan to barbecue the meat, light the charcoal about 30 minutes before cooking time, to grill, preheat the grill for about 10 minutes. Remove the lamb from the marinade and cook it for 5 to 7 minutes on each side, brushing it occasionally with any marinade remaining in the dish. Let the lamb rest for about 5 minutes before slicing it. Serve the ketchup separately.

Steaks with Grated Courgettes and a Tomato Coulis

Serves 4

Working time:
about 25
minutes

Total time: 45
minutes

Calories
280
Protein
31g
Cholesterol
75mg
Total fat
13g
Saturated fat
5g
Sodium
395mg

4	boneless steaks, trimmed, (about 140 g/4½ oz each)	4
400 g	courgettes	14 oz
1 tsp	salt	1 tsp
1 tbsp	virgin olive oil	1 tbsp
2 tbsp	chopped fresh marjoram, freshly ground black pepper lengthwise strips of courgette, for garnish (optional)	2 tbsp

	Tomato coulis	
1 tsp	virgin olive oil	1 tsp
2	garlic cloves, finely chopped	2
750 g	ripe tomatoes, skinned, seeded and finely chopped	1½ lb
1 tbsp	chopped fresh oregano,	1 tbsp
1 tsp	chopped fresh marjoram, freshly ground black pepper	1 tsp
8 cl	medium-dry white wine	3 fl oz

Trim and grate the courgettes, then transfer to a sieve set over a bowl. Stir in half a teaspoon of the salt and leave for 30 minutes.

Meanwhile, brush the steaks with the oil, rub them with half of the marjoram and sprinkle them with black pepper. Using cocktail sticks, pin the steaks into neat rounds.

To make the tomato coulis, heat the oil in a heavy-bottomed saucepan. Add the garlic and cook it for minute over medium-high heat. Add the tomatoes, herbs and some pepper. Cook until the tomatoes are reduced to a purée—about 10 minutes. Add the wine, heat the coulis through and keep warm. Preheat the grill to medium.

Season the steaks with the remaining salt and grill them for 5 to 6 minutes each side for rare to medium meat. While they are grilling, squeeze the courgette and stir-fry them with the remaining marjoram over medium low heat until they soften—about 3 minutes.

When the steaks are cooked, remove the cocktail sticks. Spread the courgette mixture evenly on top of each steak. Arrange on the plates with the tomato coulis and courgette strips and serve immediately.

Grilled Lamb with Chutney Glaze and Mint

Serves 10

Working time: about 30 minutes

Total time: about 1 hour and 15 minutes

Calories 200
Protein 23g
Cholesterol 75mg
Total fat 8g
Saturated fat 3g
Sodium 135mg

2.5 kg	leg of lamb, trimmed and boned	5 lb
1 tbsp	safflower oil	1 tbsp
¼ tbsp	salt	¼ tbsp
	freshly ground black pepper	
4 tbsp	chopped mint	4 tbsp
	mint sprigs, for garnish	

	Chutney glaze	
¼ litre	unsalted brown	8 fl oz
4 tbsp	mango chutney	4 tbsp
½ tbsp	dry mustard	½ tbsp
1 tbsp	cider vinegar	1 tbsp
½ tbsp	cornflour, mixed with 1 tbsp water	½ tbsp

Place the lamb flat on a work surface with the cut side of the meat facing upwards. Remove the membranes and tendons. Starting from the centre of the meat carefully slice horizontally into the flesh. Open out the resulting flap, then slice into the opposite side in a similar manner. The meat should be no more than 5 cm (2 inches) thick.

Preheat the grill for 10 minutes.

To make the chutney glaze, combine the stock and the mango chutney in a small saucepan and simmer over medium heat. Stir the mustard and cider vinegar into the cornflour paste and whisk into the simmering stock and chutney. Cook the glaze, stirring continuously, until it thickens. Remove the pan from the heat and set aside.

Rub both sides of the lamb with the safflower oil. Grill, turning every 5 minutes, until well browned on both sides. Sprinkle on the salt and some black pepper and brush with some of the glaze. Continue cooking the lamb, basting it frequently with the glaze for about another 10 minutes. Pour the remaining chutney glaze into a small serving bowl.

Transfer the lamb to a cutting board and sprinkle it with the chopped mint. Allow to stand for 1 minutes before carving. Serve with the remaining chutney glaze, garnished with mint sprigs.

Leg of Lamb in Spiced Apple Sauce

Serves 12

Working time:
about 45
minutes

Total time:
about 2 hours
and 25 minutes
(includes
marinating)

Calories
225
Protein
30g
Cholesterol
80mg
Total fat
9g
Saturated fat
4g
Sodium
135mg

2.5 kg	leg of lamb, trimmed and boned	**5 lb**
4 tbsp	cider vinegar	**4 tbsp**
1	onion, finely chopped	**1**
2	garlic cloves, finely chopped	**2**
1 tbsp	finely chopped fresh sage, or 1½ tsp dried sage	**1 tbsp**
½ tsp	salt	**½ tsp**
1 tbsp	freshly ground black pepper	**1 tbsp**

1 tbsp	safflower oil	**1 tbsp**
	Spiced apple sauce	
300 g	cooking apples, peeled, cored and sliced	**10 oz**
30 g	sugar	**1 oz**
2	cloves	**2**
¼ tsp	ground cinnamon	**¼ tsp**
⅛ tsp	ground allspice	**⅛ tsp**

Cook the apples gently in a heavy saucepan with 1 tablespoon of water, until soft. Drain, then purée using a sieve. Return the purée to the saucepan, add the sugar, cloves, ground cinnamon and allspice, and gently cook, stirring occasionally, until the mixture has a thick spreading consistency. Remove the cloves and set aside to cool.

Place the lamb flat on a work surface with the cut side of the meat facing upwards. Remove the membranes and tendons. Starting from the centre of the meat, slice horizontally into the flesh at one side of the leg. Open out the flap, then slice into the opposite side and

open it out in a similar manner. The meat should be no more than 5 cm (2 inches) thick.

Put the apple sauce into a large bowl and mix in the vinegar, onion, garlic, sage, salt, pepper and oil. Put the butterflied lamb into the bowl and spread the apple sauce mixture thickly all over it. Leave to marinate for about 1 hour, turning it after 30 minutes.

Preheat the grill for 10 minutes. Remove the lamb from the bowl and reserve the marinade.

Cook the lamb for 12 minutes on each side for medium-rare meat. Baste from time to time with the reserved marinade. Leave to rest for about 15 minutes, then carve and serve.

Flambéed Kebabs

Serves 6

Working time:
about 50
minutes

Total time:
about 3 hours
and 50 minutes
(includes
marinating)

Calories
255
Protein
30g
Cholesterol
75mg
Total fat
11g
Saturated fat
4g
Sodium
100mg

750 g	eye and fillet of loin, trimmed and cut into 24 cubes	1½ lb
1	large courgette, thickly sliced	1
½	green pepper, cut into strips	½
½	sweet red pepper, cut into strips	½
1	large onion, cut into 12 wedges	1
2	oranges, rind and pith removed, halved and cut into slices	2
1	firm ripe mango, peeled and cut into six pieces	1
1 tbsp	virgin olive oil	1 tbsp
4 tbsp	brandy	4 tbsp

Orange and honey marinade

1	orange, finely grated rind and strained juice only	1
3 tbsp	clear honey	3 tbsp
1	onion, finely grated	1
4	garlic cloves, crushed	4
1 tbsp	tomato paste	1 tbsp
1 tbsp	virgin olive oil	1 tbsp
1 tbsp	paprika	1 tbsp
½ tsp	salt	½ tsp
¼ tsp	cayenne pepper	¼ tsp

Mix all the marinade ingredients in a large bowl. Add the lamb and stir until coated with the marinade. Cover the bowl and allow the lamb to marinate at room temperature for 3 to 4 hours, turning it from time to time

When you are ready to assemble the kebabs, blanch the courgette and peppers in boiling water for 2 to 3 minutes. Transfer to a colander, refresh, then drain well.

Preheat the grill. Thread the lamb and pieces of courgette, pepper, onion, orange and mango on six kebab skewers. Place on the grill rack and sprinkle with olive oil. Grill for 10 to 15 minutes, turning to ensure even cooking. At the end of this time the lamb should be cooked, yet still slightly pink in the centre.

When the kebabs are ready, place them on a warmed dish. Put the brandy into a small shallow sauté pan and warm it for about 10 seconds. Standing well back, ignite the brandy in the pan and pour it, flaming, over the kebabs before serving.

Kebabs with Olive-Mint Sauce

600 g	lean lamb, trimmed and cut into 16 cubes	**1¼ lb**	**2**	onions, each cut into six wedges	**2**
30 g	mint, chopped	**1 oz**	**½**	sweet green pepper, seeded, deribbed and cut into eight	**½**
6	oil-cured black olives, stoned and finely chopped	**6**	**½**	red apple, cored and cut into eight pieces	**½**
1 tbsp	virgin olive oil	**1 tbsp**	**¼ litre**	unsalted brown or chicken stock	**8 fl oz**
½ tsp	ground allspice freshly ground black pepper	**½ tsp**			

If you plan to barbecue the lamb, light the charcoal about 30 minutes before cooking time; to grill, preheat the grill for 10 minutes.

Put the lamb into a bowl with 3 tablespoons of mint, half the olives, ½ tablespoon of the oil, ¼ teaspoon of allspice and a generous grinding of pepper. Stir the cubes to coat them with the marinade, then set the bowl aside at room temperature while you prepare the other ingredients.

Toss together the onions, green pepper, apple, 3 tablespoons of the remaining mint, the remaining olive oil and allspice and some black pepper in another bowl and set aside.

Pour the stock into a small saucepan over medium heat, then stir in the remaining olives, the remaining mint and the salt. Cook the sauce until only about 6 tablespoons remain—about 10 minutes. Remove the pan from the heat and set it aside.

Thread the lamb cubes and the vegetable and apple chunks on to four skewers. Grill the kebabs for 3 to 4 minutes on each side for medium meat. Transfer them to a platter. Reheat the sauce, pour it over the kebabs and serve immediately.

Kofta with Onion Sauce

Serves 4

Working time:
about 30
minutes

Total time:
about 40
minutes

Calories
260
Protein
27g
Cholesterol
80mg
Total fat
14g
Saturated fat
5g
Sodium
195mg

500 g	lean lamb,	1 lb
	trimmed and minced	
1	onion, finely chopped	1
60 g	pitted olives, finely chopped	2 oz
2 tbsp	chopped fresh coriander	2 tbsp
1 tbsp	Worcester sauce	1 tbsp
¼ tsp	salt	¼ tsp
	freshly ground black pepper	

Onion sauce

15 g	polyunsaturated margarine	½ oz
1	red onion, finely chopped	1
1 tsp	cumin seeds	1 tsp
2 tbsp	raspberry or cider vinegar	2 tbsp
1 tbsp	cornflour	1 tbsp
30 cl	unsalted brown stock	½ pint
⅛ tsp	salt	⅛ tsp
	freshly ground black pepper	

First, make the onion sauce. Melt the margarine in a sauté pan or heavy frying pan. Add the onion and cumin seeds, and cook them over medium heat until the onions are soft—about 4 minutes. Add the vinegar and continue cooking until the liquid reduces to a thick syrup. Mix the cornflour to a paste with 2 tablespoons of the stock. Add the remaining stock to the pan and bring it to the boil. Add the cornflour paste and stir until the sauce thickens—2 to 3 minutes. Season the sauce and keep it warm.

Combine the lamb, onion, olives, coriander, Worcester sauce, salt and some pepper in a bowl and mix thoroughly by hand. Shape the meat into 20 thick sausages, each about 4 cm (1½ inches) long. If you like, wrap eight of the sausages with pieces of caul. Carefully thread the sausages on to four long metal skewers, alternating caul-wrapped ones with plain.

Preheat the grill to high and cook the kofta for 10 minutes, turning them once. Serve the kofta hot with the onion sauce.

Leg of Lamb with Pomegranate Sauce

Serves 8

Working
time: about
30 minutes

Total time:
about 1 hour
and 30
minutes

Calories
250

Protein
30g

Cholesterol
90mg

Total fat
8g

Saturated fat
4g

Sodium
130mg

2.25 kg	leg of lamb, trimmed of fat	**4½ lb**
1 tbsp	fresh thyme	**1 tbsp**
1	pomegranate	**1**
1	lime, finely grated	**1**
1½ tbsp	redcurrant jelly	**1½ tbsp**
	grated lime rind, for garnish	
	watercress, for garnish	

Pomegranate sauce		
3	pomegranates	**3**
4 tbsp	redcurrant jelly	**4 tbsp**
1 tbsp	caster sugar	**1 tbsp**
2	limes, julienned	**2**
1½ tbsp	cornflour	**1½ tbsp**
8 cl	rose wine	**3 fl oz**

Preheat the oven to 200°C (400°F or Mark 6).

Make five incisions in the flesh of the lamb and fill with thyme. Place in a roasting pan.

Scoop out the pomegranate seeds, reserving one third for garnish. Press all the juice from the remaining seeds through a nylon sieve into a bowl. Stir in the lime rind and juice, then pour half over the lamb to coat it.

Place the joint in the oven and roast it, basting frequently, for 1 to 1¼ hours. Half way through, pour on the remaining juices.

Remove the lamb from the oven, rest it on a warm platter for about 20 minutes.

Meanwhile, make the pomegranate sauce. Scoop out the pomegranate seeds and press

out their juice through a sieve, into a saucepan. Stir in the redcurrant jelly, sugar and lime juice, then heat gently to dissolve. Cook gently for 10 minutes. Blend the cornflour with the rose wine and stir it into the sauce. Bring it to the boil and continue to cook, stirring, until the mixture thickens and clears. Add the julienned lime rind and simmer for 5 minutes more, stirring frequently. Transfer to a warmed sauceboat.

Before carving, bring the redcurrant jelly to the boil and brush it over the meat. Sprinkle the meat with the reserved pomegranate seeds; garnish with the grated lime rind and watercress. Serve the sauce separately.

Roast Leg with Herbs and Garlic

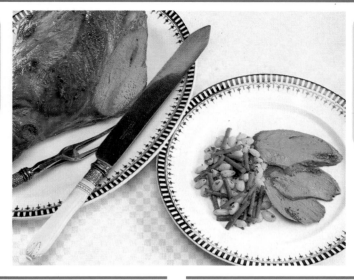

Serves 8

Working time: about 30 minutes

Total time: about 3 hours (includes marinating)

Calories 260

Protein 8g

Cholesterol 100mg

Total fat 12g

Saturated fat 5g

Sodium 195mg

2.5 kg	leg of lamb, trimmed of fat	**5 lb**
2 tbsp	chopped mixed fresh herbs (thyme, sage, rosemary, oregano), or 2 tsp mixed dried herbs	**2 tbsp**
1 tbsp	finely chopped parsley	**1 tbsp**
3	garlic cloves	**3**
1 tsp	salt	**1 tsp**
1 tbsp	virgin olive oil	**1 tbsp**

Using a small pointed knife, make 10 to 12 deep, evenly spaced incisions into the flesh of the lamb.

With a pestle and mortar, crush together the garlic cloves and salt to make a creamy paste. Add the mixed herbs and the parsley. Using your fingers or a small teaspoon, fill each incision in the lamb with the herb and garlic paste. Rub the olive oil all over the leg, then place it in a roasting pan and set it aside in a

cool place to marinate for 1 hour. Preheat the oven to 220°C (425°F or Mark 7).

Roast the leg for 15 minutes, then reduce the oven temperature to 190°C (375°F or Mark 5) and continue roasting for 50 minutes to 1 hour for rare to medium meat, basting the leg frequently with the pan juices. Transfer the leg to a serving dish, cover it loosely with foil and allow it to rest in a warm place for 20 to 30 minutes before carving.

Leg of Lamb with Pear Mustard

Serves 10

Working time:
about 1 hour

Total time:
about 2 hours
and 15
minutes

Calories
225

Protein
24g

Cholesterol
75mg

Total fat
9g

Saturated fat
3g

Sodium
430mg

2.5 kg	leg of lamb, trimmed, only the shank bone left in place	5 lb
½ tbsp	Dijon mustard	½ tbsp
1 tbsp	safflower oil	1 tbsp
¼ tsp	salt	¼ tsp
3	bunches spring onions, sliced	3
	Pear mustard	
½ tbsp	safflower oil	½ tbsp
750 g	pears, coarsely chopped	1½ lb
¼ litre	unsalted brown stock	8 fl oz
1½ tbsp	fresh lemon juice	1½ tbsp
1	shallot, finely chopped	1
1	garlic clove, finely chopped	1
1¼ tsp	salt	1¼ tsp
	freshly ground black pepper	
1½ tbsp	Dijon mustard	1½ tbsp

To make the pear mustard, gently heat the oil in a heavy saucepan. Add the pears and cook, stirring frequently, until the juice is syrupy and lightly browned. Add the stock, lemon juice, shallot, garlic, salt, some pepper and the mustard. Reduce the heat and simmer until only about 35 cl (12 fl oz) remain—15 to 20 minutes. Transfer the pear mustard to a food processor and purée it until smooth.

Meanwhile, preheat the oven to 180°C (350°F or Mark 4). Rub the Dijon mustard over the exposed inner surface of the leg. Fold the meat over, then tie securely with string. Heat the oil in a large, shallow fireproof casserole set over high heat. When the oil is hot, add the leg of

lamb and brown it evenly—about 10 minutes. Sprinkle with the salt and transfer to the oven. Roast the lamb for 20 minutes.

Remove the lamb from the oven and coat with about one third of the pear mustard, then roast it for 40 minutes more. Brush with about half of the remaining pear mustard. Increase the oven temperature to 240°C (475°F or Mark 9) and cook until the pear mustard is lightly browned—10 to 15 minutes. Rest the lamb in a warm place for 20 minutes.

Blanch the spring onions in boiling water for 1 minute, then drain. Slice the lamb and arrange on the spring onions; spoon on the remaining mustard before serving.

Leg Roasted with Ginger

Serves 10

Working time:
about 25
minutes

Total time:
about 4 hours
and 40 minutes
(includes
marinating)

Calories
185
Protein
24g
Cholesterol
75g
Total fat
7g
Saturated fat
3g
Sodium
170mg

2.5 kg	leg of lamb, trimmed of fat	5 lb
3 tbsp	finely chopped fresh ginger root	3 tbsp
3	garlic cloves, finely chopped	3
2 tsp	soy sauce	2 tsp
¼ tsp	dark sesame oil	¼ tsp
1 tsp	rice vinegar or white wine vinegar	1 tsp
6 tbsp	mirin or sweet sherry	6 tbsp
⅛ tsp	white pepper	⅛ tsp

Soy and sesame sauce		
1 tbsp	soy sauce	1 tbsp
2 tbsp	mirin or sweet sherry	2 tbsp
1 tsp	sesame seeds	1 tsp
2 tsp	rice vinegar	2 tsp
1	spring onion, trimmed and thinly sliced	1
1	small carrot, sliced	1
2 tbsp	chopped fresh ginger root	2 tbsp
12.5 cl	unsalted brown stock	4 fl oz

With a knife, lightly score the surface of the lamb in a crisscross pattern. Transfer the lamb to a shallow baking dish. Mix the ginger, garlic, soy sauce, sesame oil, vinegar, mirin or sherry and pepper in a small bowl. Pour this marinade over the lamb and refrigerate it for at least 3 hours. From time to time, baste the lamb with the marinade.

Towards the end of the marinating time,

preheat the oven to 230°C (450°F or Mark 8). Transfer the lamb to a roasting pan, reserving the marinade, and roast for 10 minutes. Reduce the oven temperature to 180°C (350°F or Mark 4) and continue roasting the lamb for 1 hour for medium-rare meat. Baste the lamb from time to time with the reserved marinade during this period. Let the lamb rest in a warm place for 20 minutes before carving it.

Garlic-Studded Lamb Shanks with Roasted Onions

4	lamb shanks, trimmed, (about 350 g/12 oz each)	4	
6	garlic cloves, each cut lengthwise into four slices	6	
½ tbsp	virgin olive oil	½ tbsp	
1 tbsp	chopped fresh rosemary,	1 tbsp	

	freshly ground black pepper		
¼ tsp	salt	¼ tsp	
4	onions, unpeeled	4	
6	carrots, cut into bâtonnets, blanched for 1 minute in boiling water	6	

Preheat the oven to 180°C (350°F or Mark 4).

With the point of a knife, make an incision in the flesh of a shank, press a garlic slice deep into the opening. Repeat the process to insert six garlic slices into each shank. Rub the shanks with the oil, then sprinkle them with the rosemary and pepper. Put the shanks in a heavy roasting pan and roast them until they are very tender—1½ to 2 hours.

After the lamb shanks have been roasting for 45 minutes, sprinkle them with the salt. Wrap the onions individually in aluminium foil and set them in the oven next to the roasting pan.

When the shanks are done, transfer them to a serving platter. Skim off the fat that has collected in the roasting pan, leaving any caramelized juices in the pan. Set the pan on the stove top over medium heat. Add the blanched carrots and cook them, stirring occasionally, for 2 minutes. Pour 4 tablespoons of water into the pan and bring the liquid to a simmer, scraping up the caramelized pan juices with a wooden spoon.

Transfer the carrots and the sauce to the platter. Unwrap the onions, cut off 1 cm (½ inch) from their tops and set them on the platter just before serving.

Leg of Lamb Stuffed with Vegetables

Serves 10

Working time:
about 40
minutes

Total time:
about 2 hours

Calories
240
Protein
25g
Cholesterol
75mg
Total fat
11g
Saturated fat
4g
Sodium
235mg

2.5 kg	leg of lamb, boned	5 lb	½ tsp	salt	½ tsp
2 tbsp	safflower oil	2 tbsp		freshly ground black pepper	
1	large carrot, julienned	1	1 tbsp	fresh thyme	1 tbsp
1	large courgette, julienned	1	¼ litre	unsalted brown stock	8 fl oz
1	large yellow squash, julienned	1	2 tbsp	finely chopped shallot	2 tbsp
12.5 cl	dry sherry	4 fl oz	1½ tbsp	cornflour, mixed with	1½ tbsp
30 g	Parmesan cheese, grated	1 oz		2 tbsp water	

Heat 1 tablespoon of the oil in a large, shallow fireproof casserole. Add the carrot and sauté, stirring often, for 2 minutes. Stir in the courgette and squash, and cook until the carrot is barely tender. Remove from the heat and add 2 tablespoons of sherry. Add the Parmesan cheese and toss the stuffing well.

Preheat the oven to 170°C (325°F or Mark 3). Spread out the lamb and season it with half the salt, some pepper and half the thyme. Spread the stuffing over the lamb and roll it up like a Swiss roll. Tie with string to secure it.

Wipe out the casserole and heat the remaining oil in it over high heat. Add the lamb roll and brown it on all sides. Put the

casserole into the oven and roast the lamb until it is tender—about 1 hour. Transfer to a platter and set it aside in a warm place.

Skim off the fat and set the casserole on the stove top over low heat. Add the stock, the remaining thyme, the shallot or onion and the remaining sherry to the casserole, then scrape the bottom to dissolve the caramelized roasting juices. Increase the heat and boil the liquid until about one third of it remains. Reduce the heat and whisk in the cornflour mixture. Cook the sauce, stirring, until it has thickened. Season the sauce.

Cut the roast into slices. Pour the sauce into a warmed sauceboat and serve it separately.

Rack of Lamb with a Spiced Parsley Crust

2	750 g (1½ lb) racks of lamb, each with 6 cutlets, chine bones removed, bone tips shortened by 5 cm (2 inches), trimmed of fat	2		¼ tsp	paprika	¼ tsp
1	small onion, finely chopped	1		½ tsp	salt	½ tsp
2	garlic cloves. crushed	2			freshly ground black pepper	
15 g	parsley, finely chopped	½ oz		1 tsp	saffron threads, soaked in 1 tsp boiling water for 1 hour	1 tsp
¼ tsp	ground cumin	¼ tsp		15 cl	white wine	¼ pint
				1 tsp	cornflour	1 tsp

In a small bowl, thoroughly mix together the onion, garlic, parsley, cumin, paprika, half the salt and some pepper. Stir in the saffron and its soaking liquid. Spread this over the outer, fleshy side of the racks and leave in a cool place, loosely covered, for 4 to 6 hours.

Preheat the oven to 220°C (425°F or Mark 7). Place the meat on a rack in a roasting pan, marinated side upwards. Roast for 25 minutes, then add the wine and 15 cl (¼ pint) of water to the roasting pan and return the meat to the oven until the crusts are turning dark round the edges—about 20 minutes. (The meat will still be slightly pink in the

centre; cover the racks with foil and roast them for a further 15 minutes if you like your lamb more thoroughly cooked.)

When the meat is cooked, transfer it to a warmed plate. Skim off the fat from the cooking liquid, and boil the liquid rapidly to reduce it slightly. Mix the cornflour with 1 tablespoon of water and stir it into the pan. Continue cooking over medium heat until the gravy thickens—2 to 3 minutes. Season the gravy with the remaining salt and some black pepper, and pour it into a warmed gravy boat. Slice the racks into cutlets and serve them with the gravy.

Guard of Honour

Serves 7

Working time: about 35 minutes

Total time: about 1 hour and 35 minutes

Calories 220

Protein 28g

Cholesterol 75mg

Total fat 9g

Saturated fat 3g

Sodium 125mg

2	850 g/(1¾ lb) racks of lamb, each with 7 cutlets, chine bones removed, bone tips shortened by 5 cm (2 inches), trimmed of fat	2
1	garlic clove, halved	1
	freshly ground black pepper	
1 tbsp	tahini	1 tbsp
1 tbsp	Dijon mustard	1 tbsp
1 tbsp	clear honey	1 tbsp
1 tbsp	mustard seeds	1 tbsp

1½ tbsp	sesame seeds	1½ tbsp
1 tbsp	chopped fresh tarragon	1 tbsp
	Red wine gravy	
12.5 cl	red wine	4 fl oz
15 cl	unsalted chicken or brown stock or water	¼ pint
1	sprig fresh tarragon	1
½ tsp	clear honey	½ tsp
¼ tsp	salt	¼ tsp

Rub the garlic clove all over the racks, and season generously with black pepper.

Mix together the tahini, mustard, honey, mustard seeds and sesame seeds. Combine 2 teaspoons of this with the chopped tarragon and spread over the inside of the racks.

Preheat the oven to 230°C (450°F or Mark 8). Assemble the guard by interlocking the exposed rib bone tips. Tie with string. Cover the exposed bone tips with a single layer of aluminium foil.

Spread the remaining tahini-mustard paste over the outside of the assembled guard. Place in a roasting pan. Roast the lamb for 50 minutes to 1 hour and 10 minutes for rare to medium meat. Transfer to a warm platter, remove strings, and set it aside to rest.

Skim off the fat from the liquid in the roasting pan and transfer the pan to the stove top. Add the wine and boil it over high heat, stirring to scrape up any sediment. Add the stock, tarragon, honey and salt and boil to reduce by about half. Strain the gravy into a sauce boat. Carve the guard at the table.

Chops Stuffed with Walnuts and Parsley

Serves 4

Working time:
about 20
minutes

Total time:
about 40
minutes

Calories
280
Protein
23g
Cholesterol
65mg
Total fat
14g
Saturated fat
5g
Sodium
215mg

4	loin chops, trimmed (about 125 g/4 oz each)	4
2 tsp	safflower oil	2 tsp
1	onion, chopped	1
12.5 cl	unsalted chicken stock	4 fl oz
3 tbsp	currants	3 tbsp
45 g	fresh breadcrumbs	1½ oz
2 tsp	chopped parsley	2 tsp
2 tbsp	chopped shelled walnuts	2 tbsp
1 tsp	chopped fresh thyme	1 tsp
¼ tsp	salt	¼ tsp
	freshly ground black pepper	

First prepare the stuffing. Gently heat 1 teaspoon of the oil in a frying pan. Add the onion and cook until translucent. Add the stock and currants and bring the liquid to a simmer. Remove from the heat and cover. Let stand until the currants have plumped up—about 5 minutes. Stir in the breadcrumbs, parsley, walnuts, thyme, ⅛ teaspoon of the salt and some pepper and set aside.

Preheat the oven to 200°C (400°F or Mark 6). Lay out the chops. Insert a small knife horizontally into each chop in turn on the right-hand side, near the end of the bone that divides the fillet from the eye. Cut towards the eye, but make sure that the knife does not emerge on the far side. Rotate the knife to

create a pocket within the flesh of the eye. Fill the pockets with the stuffing mixture. Fold the long, thin apron of the chop to cover the opening of the pocket, and secure the apron to the fillet with a cocktail stick.

Heat the remaining teaspoon of oil in a shallow fireproof casserole over medium-high heat. Place the chops in the oil and lightly brown them on one side—1 to 2 minutes. Turn the chops over and season them with the remaining ⅛ teaspoon of salt and some more pepper. Put the casserole into the oven and bake the chops for 15 to 20 minutes.

Remove the casserole from the oven and let the chops rest in a warm place for 5 minutes. Remove the cocktail sticks before serving.

Lamb with Hazelnut Sauce

Serves 6

Working (and total) time: about 30 minutes

Calories 175
Protein 23g
Cholesterol 65mg
Total fat 14g
Saturated fat 5g
Sodium 200mg

2	racks of lamb, boned (about 600 g/1¼ lb each), the flap of meat that extends from the eye removed	**2**
45 cl	unsalted brown or chicken stock	**¾ pint**

12.5 cl	dry white wine	**4 fl oz**
½ tsp	salt	**½ tsp**
	freshly ground black pepper	
175 g	turnips, peeled and finely diced	**6 oz**
60 g	shelled hazelnuts, toasted and chopped	**2 oz**

Preheat the oven to 230°C (450°F or Mark 8).

To make the sauce put the stock and wine in a saucepan and boil rapidly until only half of the liquid remains—8 to 10 minutes. Season with ¼ teaspoon of the salt and some black pepper. Add the turnips to the reduced stock and simmer them until they are just tender—about 5 minutes—then remove the pan from the heat and set it aside.

While the sauce is cooking, brush a heavy frying pan with a little oil. Set the pan over high heat, then quickly seal the meat and transfer it to a roasting pan. Season the meat with the remaining salt and some black pepper. Roast the lamb for 5 to 10 minutes for rare to medium meat·

Just before the meat is ready, return the sauce to the heat. Stir in the chopped hazelnuts and heat the sauce through.

Carve the lamb and arrange slices on six plates. Serve with the sauce spooned over the meat.

Editor's Note: To toast hazelnuts, put them on a baking sheet in a preheated 130°C (350°F or Mark 4) oven for 10 minutes.

Loin with Juniper Berry Sauce

2	loins of lamb (about 1 kg/2¼ lb each), boned and trimmed of fat, fillet reserved	**2**
1 litre	unsalted brown or chicken stock	**1¾ pints**
30 cl	dry Madeira	**½ pint**
4 tsp	redcurrant jelly	**4 tsp**
4 tsp	juniper berries, coarsely crushed with a pestle and mortar	**4 tsp**
1 tsp	virgin olive oil	**1 tsp**

Preheat the oven to 220°C (425°F or Mark 7).

Put the stock, Madeira and redcurrant jelly in a heavy-bottomed saucepan and boil them over high heat until the liquid is reduced to about ½ litre (16 fl oz). Add half the juniper berries and continue boiling until the stock has further reduced to about 30 cl (½ pint), then remove the pan from the heat and set it aside.

Meanwhile, brush the eyes of loin with the oil, sprinkle the meat with the remaining juniper berries and place it in a roasting pan.

Roast the meat on the middle shelf of the oven for 12 minutes. Turn off the heat and leave the lamb in the pan on the floor of the oven for 10 minutes.

Transfer the lamb to a warmed serving dish, cover the dish and set it aside in a warm place. Skim off any fat from the juices in the pan and pour the remaining juices into the juniper berry sauce. Reheat the sauce, pour some of it round the lamb to moisten it and pour the rest into a warmed sauce boat. Serve immediately.

Loin on a Bed of Green Leaves

Serves 8

Working time:
about 40
minutes

Total time:
about 1 hour
and 45
minutes

Calories
235
Protein
24g
Cholesterol
75mg
Total fat
12g
Saturated fat
4g
Sodium
195mg

2	loins (about 1 kg/2¼ lb each), trimmed of fat	**2**
1 tbsp	virgin olive oil	**1 tbsp**
1 tbsp	grainy mustard	**1 tbsp**
⅛ tsp	salt	**⅛ tsp**
	freshly ground black pepper	
2	garlic cloves, finely chopped	**2**
25 g	fresh wholemeal breadcrumbs	**¾ oz**
1 tbsp	chopped parsley	**1 tbsp**
1 tsp	chopped fresh thyme	**1 tsp**
1 tsp	chopped fresh rosemary	**1 tsp**

Wilted green leaf salad

1 tbsp	virgin olive oil	**1 tbsp**
2	spring onions, trimmed and chopped	**2**
500 g	dandelion greens or spinach, stemmed and washed	**1 lb**
1	bunch watercress, trimmed, washed and dried	**1**
16	cherry tomatoes, halved	**16**
1 tbsp	red wine vinegar	**1 tbsp**
⅛ tsp	salt	**⅛ tsp**
	freshly ground black pepper	

Put the lamb in a roasting pan bone side down. Combine 1 teaspoon of the oil, the mustard, salt, some pepper and half of the garlic. Rub on the lamb and leave for 1 hour.

Preheat the oven to 220°C (425°F or Mark 7). Roast the lamb until it has browned—25 to 35 minutes for rare to medium meat.

Mix together the breadcrumbs, parsley, thyme, rosemary, the remaining garlic and some pepper. Sprinkle the breadcrumb mixture over the lamb; dribble the remaining 2 teaspoons

of oil over the breadcrumbs. Continue roasting until the breadcrumbs have browned. Keep the lamb warm while you make the salad.

For the salad, heat the oil in a heavy frying pan over medium-high heat. Add the spring onions and sauté for 45 seconds, then add the greens, watercress, tomatoes and vinegar. Toss the vegetables until the greens are slightly wilted—about 30 seconds. Remove the pan from the heat and season the salad.

Carve the lamb into 16 pieces and serve.

Braised Lamb with Mango

Serves 4

Working time:
about 30
minutes

Total time:
about 7 hours
and 30 minutes
(includes
marinating)

Calories
300
Protein
45g
Cholesterol
75mg
Total fat
10g
Saturated fat
4g
Sodium
320mg

500 g	làmb slices, cut from the fillet end of the leg, trimmed of fat and cut into long strips	**1 lb**
30 cl	plain low fat yogurt	**½ pint**
1 tsp	chopped ginger root	**1 tsp**
1 tbsp	ground coriander	**1 tbsp**
1 tsp	ground cumin	**1 tsp**
2 tsp	safflower oil	**2 tsp**
1	onion, finely sliced	**1**

1	garlic clove, crushed	**1**
2 tsp	coriander seeds, crushed	**2 tsp**
1 tbsp	cornflour	**1 tbsp**
12.5 cl	unsalted chicken stock	**4 fl oz**
1	bay leaf	**1**
⅛ tsp	powdered saffron or turmeric	**⅛ tsp**
¾ tsp	salt	**¾ tsp**
2	mangoes	**2**
4	large fresh coriander leaves	**4**

Mix together the yogurt, ginger, ground coriander and cumin, then stir in the strips of lamb, coating them. Cover and leave to marinate in the refrigerator for at least 6 hours.

In a heavy-bottomed fireproof casserole, heat the oil and stir in the onion and garlic. Cook them over low heat for 1 minute, then add the crushed coriander seeds and sauté until the seeds begin to pop. Mix the cornflour with a tablespoon of the lamb marinade. Stir the cornflour mixture into the rest of the marinade. Transfer the meat and its marinade to the casserole and continue

cooking gently for 1 minute. Add the stock, bay leaf, saffron or turmeric, and salt. Cover the casserole and simmer the stew over low heat until the meat is tender—about 1 hour.

Peel the mangoes; cut two thin slices from one of them and reserve these for a garnish. Remove the stones and cut the flesh into 1 cm (½ inch) cubes. Add the mango cubes to the lamb and simmer the casserole over low heat for a further 5 minutes.

To serve, coarsely chop the coriander leaves and sprinkle them over the lamb. Garnish with the reserved slices of mango.

Lamb with Puréed Asparagus and Jerusalem Artichokes

Serves 6

Working time:
about 1 hour

Total time:
about 2 hours
and 30
minutes

Calories
225
Protein
30g
Cholesterol
80mg
Total fat
9g
Saturated fat
4g
Sodium
270mg

750 g	lean lamb, trimmed, and cut into strips	**1½ lb**		**500 g**	Jerusalem artichokes	**1 lb**
500 g	asparagus, trimmed and peeled	**1 lb**		**4 tsp**	fresh lemon juice	**4 tsp**
1 tsp	salt	**1 tsp**		**60 g**	watercress, blanched for 30 seconds and chopped	**2 oz**
½ tbsp	safflower oil	**½ tbsp**		**¼ tsp**	white pepper	**¼ tsp**
3	shallots, halved	**3**		**3 tbsp**	thick Greek yogurt	**3 tbsp**

Cut the tips off the asparagus spears. Cook the stems in boiling water with half a teaspoon of salt, until soft—about 15 minutes. Remove the stems, drain, and set them aside; strain and reserve the cooking liquid.

Heat the oil in a frying pan and cook the shallots until soft. Transfer to a casserole. Increase the heat and lightly brown the lamb in two batches, transferring each batch to the casserole. Pour the reserved asparagus cooking liquid over the meat and shallots. The liquid should cover the lamb. Simmer until the meat is tender—about 1 hour.

Meanwhile, put 1 teaspoon of the lemon juice into a pan with 1 litre (1¾ pints) of water. Prepare the artichokes, dropping them into

the water immediately. Bring the water to the boil and cook until tender—20 to 30 minutes. Drain, and purée in a blender. Purée and sieve the asparagus stems. Set the purées aside.

Skim off any fat from the casserole and remove the meat and shallots. Bring the liquid in the casserole to the boil, then add the asparagus tips and cook until they are just tender—about 5 minutes. Remove the tips with a slotted spoon and keep them warm.

Stir in the purées and the watercress and season with the remaining lemon juice and salt and the white pepper. Reheat the meat in the sauce. Add the asparagus tips and swirl the yogurt on the top.

Indian Lamb with Spinach

Serves 6

Working time:
about 50
minutes

Total time:
about 2 hours

Calories
275
Protein
37g
Cholesterol
75mg
Total fat
9g
Saturated fat
4g
Sodium
400mg

500 g	lean lamb trimmed and cut into cubes	1 lb
1	large onion, finely chopped	1
4 tsp	ground coriander	4 tsp
1 tbsp	mustard seeds	1 tbsp
2 tsp	ground cumin	2 tsp
1 tsp	chili powder	1 tsp
1 tsp	ground turmeric	1 tsp

20 cl	plain low fat yogurt	7 fl oz
2.5 cm	piece fresh ginger root finely chopped	1 inch
3	garlic cloves, crushed	3
1 kg	fresh spinach, trimmed and torn into pieces	2 lb
$\frac{1}{4}$ tsp	salt	$\frac{1}{4}$ tsp

Brush a heavy, non-stick fireproof casserole or saucepan with oil, add the onion and soften it over medium-high heat for 2 to 3 minutes, stirring constantly. Stir in the lamb cubes, coriander, mustard seeds, cumin, chili powder and turmeric and mix all the ingredients thoroughly together. Add 1 tablespoon of the yogurt and cook over high heat, stirring the meat continuously until all of the yogurt is absorbed—3 to 5 minutes. Add the rest of the yogurt, 1 tablespoon at a time, stirring constantly after each addition until the yogurt is completely absorbed.

Stir in the ginger and garlic, add just enough water to cover the meat and bring the liquid to the boil. Cover the casserole, reduce the heat and simmer until the lamb is tender—about 1 hour.

When the meat is cooked, increase the heat to medium and add the spinach in batches, stirring each batch until it is wilted. When all the spinach is incorporated cook the stew, uncovered, over high heat to evaporate any excess liquid—about 5 minutes. Add the salt just before serving.

Navarin with Mustard Croûtons

Serves 4

Working time:
about 45
minutes

Total time:
about 7 hours
(includes
chilling)

Calories
430
Protein
35g
Cholesterol
75mg
Total fat
9g
Saturated fat
4g
Sodium
600mg

500 g	lean stewing lamb, trimmed and cut into cubes	**1 lb**
1 tbsp	plain flour	**1 tbsp**
60 cl	unsalted brown stock	**1 pint**
1	onion, sliced	**1**
2 tbsp	tomato paste	**2 tbsp**
2	fresh bay leaves	**2**
1 tsp	chopped fresh thyme	**1 tsp**
¼ tsp	salt	**¼ tsp**

	freshly ground black pepper	
250 g	turnips, peeled	**8 oz**
250 g	tiny new potatoes, scrubbed	**8 oz**
250 g	courgettes	**8 oz**
250 g	cherry tomatoes, skinned	**8 oz**
1	small baguette	**1**
2	garlic cloves	**2**
4 tsp	grainy mustard	**4 tsp**

Preheat the oven to 190°C (375°F or Mark 5). Toss the meat in the flour. Heat a fireproof casserole over a high heat and sear the meat, on all sides. Stir in the stock, onion, tomato paste, bay leaves, thyme, salt and some pepper. Bring the mixture to the boil. Cover, transfer to the oven and cook for 50 minutes.

Cut the turnips into cubes and add them with the potatoes to the casserole. Return it to the oven for a further 50 minutes. Remove from the oven, allow to cool, then transfer it to a bowl and refrigerate it until a layer of fat forms on the surface—4 hours or overnight.

Preheat the oven to 190°C (375°F or Mark 5). Discard the layer of fat, remove the bay leaves and transfer the stew to a clean casserole. Cut the courgettes and stir them into the casserole with the tomatoes. Cut the baguette diagonally into 1 cm (½ inch) slices. Halve the cloves of garlic and rub their cut surfaces all over the bread. Spread one side of the bread slices with mustard and arrange them, mustard side up, around the edge of the casserole. Cook the navarin, uncovered, until it is heated through and the bread is crisp—about 25 minutes.

Old-Fashioned Lamb and Celery

Serves 8

Working time: about 45 minutes

Total time: about 1 hour and 30 minutes

Calories 325
Protein 33g
Cholesterol 90mg
Total fat 13g
Saturated fat 4g
Sodium 225mg

1 kg	lean lamb, trimmed and cut into cubes	**2 lb**
60 cl	unsalted chicken or veal stock	**1 pint**
500 g	baby onions, peeled	**1 lb**
500 g	button mushrooms, wiped and trimmed	**1 lb**
8	sticks celery, sliced	**8**

2 tbsp	cornflour	**2 tbsp**
60 cl	red wine	**1 pint**
2	fresh rosemary sprigs	**2**
8	anchovy fillets, drained, dried on paper towels and finely chopped freshly ground black pepper	**8**
16	shelled walnut halves, toasted	**16**

Heat a large non-stick frying pan and quickly brown the cubes of meat on all sides. Transfer the meat to a fireproof casserole, add the stock and simmer, covered, for 30 minutes.

Meanwhile, dry-fry the onions in the frying pan over medium heat for 1 minute. Add the mushrooms and celery and continue cooking, stirring frequently, until the vegetables are golden—3 to 4 minutes.

Mix the cornflour with a little of the red wine and stir this into the stock in the casserole. Add the rest of the wine and bring the liquid to the boil, stirring all the time. Add the dry-fried vegetables, together with the rosemary sprigs, chopped anchovies and

some pepper, then cover the casserole and simmer the stew until the meat is tender—about 45 minutes.

About 5 minutes before the end of the cooking time, stir in the toasted walnut halves. There should be just enough liquid left to cover the meat; if there is too much liquid, transfer some of it to a saucepan over a high heat, reduce it, then return it to the casserole. Serve the stew hot.

Editor's Note: To toast walnuts, place them on a baking sheet in a 180°C (350°F or Mark 4) oven for 10 minutes.

Braised Steaks with a Pumpkin Purée

Serves 4

Working time:
about 30
minutes

Total time:
about 2 hours
and 15
minutes

Calories
370
Protein
30g
Cholesterol
90mg
Total fat
13g
Saturated fat
5g
Sodium
370mg

4	boneless lamb steaks (about 125 g/4 oz each), cut from the fillet end of the leg, trimmed of fat	**4**
1 tsp	safflower oil	**1 tsp**
½ tsp	saffron threads	**½ tsp**
¼ tsp	sea salt	**¼ tsp**
30 cl	unsalted chicken stock	**½ pint**
1 kg	pumpkin, peeled and cut into 4 cm 1½ inch) cubes	**2 lb**
4	fresh oregano sprigs	**4**
½ tsp	salt	**½ tsp**
¼ tsp	white pepper	**¼ tsp**
4 tbsp	thick Greek yogurt, mixed with 1 tbsp water	**4 tbsp**
30 g	shelled walnuts, quartered and toasted, for garnish fresh oregano leaves, for garnish	**1 oz**

Secure the steaks with short skewers to form neat rounds. Heat the oil in a wide, heavy frying pan over high heat and brown the steak for about 5 minutes. Transfer the meat to a large fireproof casserole.

Grind the saffron with the sea salt in a mortar. Bring the stock to the boil, dissolve the saffron and salt in the stock and pour it over the meat. Add the pumpkin and tne oregano sprigs to the casserole and simmer gently, partly covered, until the meat is tender—about 1¾ hours. Remove the scum or fat which rises to the surface.

Lift the steaks out of the casserole and remove the skewers, keep the steaks warm while preparing the sauce. Discard the oregano Puree the pumpkin with a little of the stock in a blender, then blend in the remaining stock. Reheat the pumpkin purée and season it with the ½ teaspoon of salt and the pepper. Spoon it on to four warm plates and place a steak in the centre of each. Drop small spoonfuls of yogurt into the purée surrounding the meat and draw a pattern using a fork. Garnish with the walnuts and oregano leaves.

Mexican Lamb

Serves 8

Working time:
about 45
minutes

Total time:
about 1 hour
and 45
minutes

Calories
220
Protein
24g
Cholesterol
75mg
Total fat
11g
Saturated fat
3g
Sodium
210mg

1.25 kg	lean lamb, trimmed and cut into cubes	**2½ lb**
2 tbsp	virgin olive oil	**2 tbsp**
5	garlic cloves, finely chopped	**5**
1	green chili pepper, seeded, deribbed and finely chopped	**1**
¼ tsp	grated nutmeg	**¼ tsp**
1 tsp	cumin seeds	**1 tsp**
1	onion, cut into cubes	**1**

1	sweet green pepper, seeded, deribbed and diced	**1**
2	large ripe tomatoes, skinned, seeded and cut into 1 cm (½ inch) pieces	**2**
¼ litre	unsalted brown or chicken stock	**8 fl oz**
½ tsp	salt	**½ tsp**
1½ tbsp	cocoa powder	**1½ tbsp**

Heat 1 tablespoon of the olive oil in a large, heavy sauté pan set over high heat. Add half of the lamb cubes and sauté them until they are browned on all sides—5 to 7 minutes. With a slotted spoon, remove the cubes from the pan and transfer them to a bowl. Return the pan to the heat; pour in ½ tablespoon of the remaining oil, and brown the rest of the lamb cubes. Set them aside also.

Add the remaining ½ tablespoon of oil to the pan and return it to the heat. Add the chopped garlic, chili pepper and cumin seeds, and cook the mixture until the garlic is lightly browned—about 1 minute. Add the onion cubes, sweet green pepper, tomatoes, stock, salt and grated nutmeg, and bring the mixture to a simmer. Return the lamb cubes and their juices to the sauté pan, then stir in the cocoa powder. Simmer the stew, stirring occasionally, until the meat is very tender and the sauce has thickened—about 1 hour. Remove the stew from the heat and let it stand for about 10 minutes before serving.

Lamb Shank with Chick-Peas

Serves 6

Working time: about 30 minutes

Total time: about 3 hours and 20 minutes (includes soaking)

Calories 240
Protein 25g
Cholesterol 50mg
Total fat 6g
Saturated fat 2g
Sodium 185mg

1.25 kg	leg of lamb, shank end	**2½ lb**
500 g	dried chick-peas, picked over	**8 oz**
1½ litre	unsalted brown stock	**16 fl oz**
¼ tsp	salt	**¼ tsp**
	freshly ground black pepper	
¼ tsp	ground coriander	**¼ tsp**
1	onion, quartered	**1**
3	garlic cloves, thinly sliced	**3**
1 tbsp	tomato paste	**1 tbsp**
1½ tsp	fresh thyme, or ½ tsp dried thyme	**1½ tsp**
1 tbsp	fresh lemon juice	**1 tbsp**

Rinse the chick-peas under running water, then put them into a large, heavy-bottomed saucepan, and cover well with water. Cover the pan, leaving the lid ajar, and slowly bring the liquid to the boil over medium-low heat. Boil for 2 minutes, then turn off the heat and soak them for at least 1 hour.

Meanwhile, place the lamb in a large saucepan with 2 litres (3½ pints) of water. Bring the water to the boil and blanch the meat for 3 minutes. Drain, transfer it to a plate, and set the plate aside.

Drain the chick-peas and return them to the saucepan. Pour in 1 litre (1¾ pints) of water and the stock, and bring to the boil over high heat. Add the blanched shanks and the salt, some pepper and the coriander. Reduce the heat and simmer for 45 minutes.

Add the onion, garlic, tomato paste, thyme and lemon juice to the lamb and chick-peas, and stir to combine them. Simmer the mixture until the lamb is very tender—1 to 1½ hours. Remove the meat from the pot and transfer it to a plate. Let it stand until it is cool enough to handle. Skim the fat from the surface of the chick-pea mixture and keep it warm. Remove the meat from the shank bone and cut it into 1 cm (½ inch) pieces; discard the bone. Return the lamb pieces to the pot. This dish can be served immediately or prepared in advance. To reheat, add 12.5 cl (4 fl oz) of water, bring to a simmer and cook for 10 minutes.

Lamb Shanks with Orange and Cinnamon

Serves 2

Working time: about 45 minutes

Total time: about 2 hours and 10 minutes

Calories 285
Protein 20g
Cholesterol 50mg
Total fat 10g
Saturated fat 2g
Sodium 255mg

2	lamb shanks (about 350 g/ 12 oz each), trimmed of fat	2
30 g	flour	1 oz
	freshly ground black pepper	
1 tbsp	chopped fresh oregano, or 1 tsp dried oregano	1 tbsp
1 tbsp	safflower oil	1 tbsp
1	small onion, chopped	1
1	garlic clove, finely chopped	1
60 ml	red wine	2 fl oz
2 tbsp	fresh orange juice	2 tbsp
$\frac{1}{8}$ tsp	salt	$\frac{1}{8}$ tsp
1	bay leaf	1
$\frac{1}{2}$	cinnamon stick, or $\frac{1}{8}$ tsp ground cinnamon	$\frac{1}{2}$
150 g	pearl onions, blanched for 2 mins in boiling water, peeled	5 oz
250 g	carrots, cut crosswise	8 oz
$\frac{1}{2}$ tbsp	julienned orange rind	$\frac{1}{2}$ tbsp
2 tbsp	finely chopped parsley	2 tbsp

Put the flour, some pepper and half of the oregano into a large plastic bag. Add the shanks and shake the bag to coat the meat with the mixture.

Heat the oil in a large, heavy sauté pan over medium-high heat. Sauté the shanks, turning them from time to time, until they have browned. Add the chopped onion, reduce the heat and cover the pan. Cook for 5 minutes, stirring occasionally.

Increase the heat to medium high and add the garlic, wine, orange juice and 350 ml (12 fl oz) of water. Bring the liquid to a simmer, scraping the bottom of the pan with a wooden spoon to dissolve any caramelized juices. Add the salt, bay leaf, cinnamon and the remaining oregano. Reduce the heat, cover, and simmer the meat until it is barely tender—about 1½ hours.

Skim any fat from the surface of the liquid; add the pearl onions, carrots and orange rind. Simmer the lamb, partially covered, until the vegetables are tender—about 30 minutes.

Skim off any more fat, stir in the chopped parsley, and serve the lamb with the vegetables and the sauce.

Braised Leg of Lamb with Mustard Seeds

Serves 8

Working time: about 40 minutes

Total time: about 3 hours

Calories 205
Protein 20g
Cholesterol 55mg
Total fat 7g
Saturated fat 2g
Sodium 155mg

1.5 kg	leg of lamb, shank end, trimmed	3 lb	$\frac{1}{2}$ tsp	celery seeds	$\frac{1}{2}$ tsp	
1 tbsp	virgin olive oil	1 tbsp	$\frac{1}{4}$ tsp	salt	$\frac{1}{4}$ tsp	
35 cl	stout	12 fl oz		freshly ground black pepper		
$\frac{1}{4}$ litre	unsalted brown stock	8 fl oz	4	bay leaves	4	
2	onions, quartered	2	3	whole cloves	3	
3	garlic cloves	3	500 g	swede, peeled and cubed	1 lb	
1 tsp	mustard seeds	1 tsp	1 kg	green cabbage, quartered and cored	2 lb	

Heat the oil in a large, fireproof casserole. Add the lamb and brown it on all sides. Pour in the beer and the stock, then add the onions, garlic, mustard seeds, celery seeds, salt and some pepper. Tie up the bay leaves and cloves in a piece of muslin and add them to the casserole. Bring the liquid to the boil, then reduce the heat to maintain a simmer.

Cover the casserole, leaving the lid slightly ajar, and braise the lamb for about 1¼ hours, turning during the cooking. Add the swede cubes and continue braising the lamb until it is tender— approximately 30 minutes more.

While the swede is cooking, pour enough water into a large pan to fill it about 2.5 cm (1 inch) deep. Using a vegetable steamer cook the cabbage until it is tender.

Transfer the cabbage to a large platter and cover it. Remove the lamb from the casserole and set it on a carving board. Transfer the swede and onions to a bowl and cover.

Remove the bay leaves and cloves from the casserole. Reduce the sauce over high heat until only about ¼ litre (8 fl oz) of it remains— about 10 minutes. Carve the lamb and arrange the slices on the cabbage. Surround the lamb with the swede and onions, then pour the sauce over the top. Serve at once.

Lamb Poached in Buttermilk

Serves 4

Working time: about 15 minutes

Total time: about 1 hour and 15 minutes

Calories 480
Protein 34g
Cholesterol 80mg
Total fat 13g
Saturated fat 3g
Sodium 410mg

600 g	lean lamb, trimmed and cut into cubes	1¼ lb
2 tsp	safflower oil	2 tsp
1	sweet green pepper, seeded, deribbed and cut into squares	1
1	onion, cut into cubes	1
¼ tsp	salt	¼ tsp
	white pepper	
1	large carrot, cut into 2.5cm (1 inch) pieces	1
2 tsp	caraway seeds	2 tsp
	cayenne pepper	
35 cl	unsalted chicken stock	12 fl oz
¼ litre	buttermilk	8 fl oz
1½ tbsp	cornflour	1½ tbsp
250 g	dried egg noodles	8 oz

Heat the oil in a large heavy-bottomed saucepan set over medium heat. Add the green pepper squares and onion cubes, and cook them, stirring frequently, until the onion is translucent—about 5 minutes. Add the lamb, salt, some white pepper, the carrot, caraway seeds, a pinch of cayenne pepper and the chicken stock; bring the liquid to a simmer. Mix the buttermilk and cornflour in a small bowl, then whisk them into the simmering liquid. Cover the saucepan, leaving the lid slightly ajar, and simmer the lamb until it is tender—about 45 minutes.

Add the noodles to 3 litres (5 pints) of boiling water with 1½ teaspoons of salt. Start testing the noodles after 6 minutes and cook them until they are al dente. Drain the noodles and transfer them to a serving dish. Top the noodles with the lamb and serve at once.

Salade Niçoise

Serves 6

Working time:
about 50
minutes

Total time:
about 1 hour
and 15
minutes

Calories
330
Protein
31g
Cholesterol
75mg
Total fat
14g
Saturated fat
6g
Sodium
270mg

1 kg	loin of lamb, trimmed	**2¼ lb**
500 g	small new potatoes	**1 lb**
3	tomatoes, sliced	**3**
250 g	French beans, topped and tailed	**8 oz**
½	cucumber	**½**
	freshly ground black pepper	
1	round lettuce, washed	**1**
6	black olives, stoned and halved	**6**
3	anchovy fillets, washed and chopped	**3**

	Herb vinaigrette	
2	garlic cloves, crushed	**2**
1 tsp	Dijon mustard	**1 tsp**
¼ tsp	salt	**¼ tsp**
3 tbsp	fresh lemon juice	**3 tbsp**
½ tbsp	fresh chopped oregano	**½ tbsp**
1 tbsp	virgin olive oil	**1 tbsp**
1 tbsp	chopped parsley	**1 tbsp**
1 tbsp	chopped fresh basil	**1 tbsp**

Preheat the oven to 230 C (450 F or Mark 8). Season the loin all over with the pepper, place it in a roasting pan and cook for 45 minutes to 1 hour. Allow it to cool.

Boil the potatoes until tender—20 to 25 minutes—then drain them and leave to cool. Cook the beans in boiling water until they are tender but still crisp—drain, rinse, then dry. Leave to cool.

Peel the cucumber and halve lengthwise. Scoop out the seeds and discard, then slice each half.

To make the vinaigrette, mix together the garlic, mustard and salt in a bowl, then whisk in the lemon juice and olive oil. Stir in the chopped parsley, basil and oregano, and set aside.

Cut the loin off the bone and cut the meat into short strips. Put these in a bowl and coat with the vinaigrette. Add the potatoes, French beans, cucumber and tomatoes and toss.

Line a salad bowl with lettuce leaves before adding the tossed salad. Sprinkle with chopped anchovies and add the olives.

Roast Lamb and Pink Grapefruit Salad

Serves 8

Working time: about 35 minutes

Total time: about 2 hours and 50 minutes (includes cooling)

Calories 265

Protein 30g

Cholesterol 75mg

Total fat 14g

Saturated fat 6g

Sodium 170mg

2 kg	leg of lamb, trimmed of fat	4 lb
2	pink grapefruits	2
1 tbsp	safflower oil	1 tbsp
1 tbsp	Dijon mustard	1 tbsp
1 tbsp	dry mustard	1 tbsp
1 tbsp	clear honey	1 tbsp
	freshly ground black pepper	
400 g	mixed salad leaves, such as oakleaf, red lollo and watercress	14 oz

Mustard-honey dressing

1 tsp	Dijon mustard	1 tsp
1 tsp	dry mustard	1 tsp
1 tsp	clear honey	1 tsp
$\frac{1}{2}$ tsp	salt	$\frac{1}{2}$ tsp
$\frac{1}{4}$ tsp	white pepper	$\frac{1}{4}$ tsp
1 tsp	wine vinegar	1 tsp
1 tbsp	safflower oil	1 tbsp
1 tbsp	hazelnut oil	1 tbsp

Preheat the oven to 230°C (450°F or Mark 8). Finely grate the rind of one grapefruit into a small bowl. Add the safflower oil, Dijon mustard, dry mustard and honey. Mix well and spread over the lamb. Season generously.

Put the lamb in a roasting pan and cook it for 15 minutes. Reduce the heat to 180°C (350°F or Mark 4) and continue to roast the lamb until it is cooked—1 to 1¼ hours for rare to medium-rare meat. Then rest the lamb at room temperature for at least 1 hour; if serving it later in the day, chill it as soon as it has reached to room temperature.

Remove the skin and white pith from both grapefruits. Holding them over a bowl, carefully remove the segments by cutting between the flesh and the connecting membrane. Keep the segments separate from the juice.

To make the dressing, whisk together the mustards, honey, salt, white pepper and wine vinegar. Whisk in the oils, and finally 4 tablespoons of the grapefruit juice. Toss the salad leaves in the dressing. Carve the meat and serve the slices alternated with the grapefruit segments, accompanied by the salad leaves.

Gyros

Serves 12

Working time:
about 45
minutes

Total time:
about 2 hours
(includes
marinating)

Calories
360

Protein
35g

Cholesterol
80mg

Total fat
10g

Saturated fat
3g

Sodium
330mg

1.25 kg	boneless leg of lamb, sliced	**2½ lb**	**1 tbsp**	safflower oil	**1 tbsp**
500 g	beef rump steak, sliced	**1 lb**	**12**	pitta breads, cut in half	**12**
1	lemon, juice only	**1**	**1**	cos lettuce, shredded	
3	garlic cloves, finely chopped	**3**	**3**	large ripe tomatoes, chopped	**3**
3 tbsp	finely chopped fresh oregano	**3 tbsp**		**Tzatziki**	
½ tsp	ground coriander	**½ tsp**	**¼ litre**	plain low-fat yogurt	**8 fl oz**
½ tsp	salt	**½ tsp**	**1**	cucumber, peeled	**1**
	freshly ground black pepper		**4 tbsp**	finely cut fresh dill	**4 tbsp**
2	egg whites	**2**	**½ tsp**	distilled white vinegar	**½ tsp**
½ tbsp	paprika	**½ tbsp**	**⅛ tsp**	salt	**⅛ tsp**

Pound the lamb and beef to a thickness of about 3 mm (⅛ inch). Transfer to two bowls.

Mix the lemon juice, garlic, oregano, coriander, salt and some pepper. Divide this between the bowls, and toss well. In another bowl, beat the egg whites with the paprika.

To assemble the gyros, brush a slice of beef with some of the egg white mixture. Top the beef with two slices of lamb and brush them with egg white mixture. Continue stacking and brushing the slices, pressing down to compact them. Insert two metal skewers, then

lay the stack on its side. Let stand at room temperature for 1 to 2 hours before cooking.

To make the tzatziki, purée the ingredients, transfer to a bowl and chill.

When the barbecue coals are hot, bank them against the sides. Place a foil drip pan in the centre of the grate and set the rack in place. Brush the gyros with the oil and lay it on centre of the rack. Cook the gyros, turning it often to ensure that it cooks evenly.

Remove the gyros from the rack and let it rest before slicing and serving.

Warm Mediterranean Lamb Salad

Serves 4

Working time: about 35 minutes

Total time: about 2 hours and 15 minutes

Calories 280
Protein 32g
Cholesterol 95mg
Total fat 13g
Saturated fat 5g
Sodium 350mg

1.25 kg	leg of lamb, shank end, trimmed	2½ lb	¾ tsp	dry mustard	¾ tsp
¼ tsp	salt	¼ tsp	7.5 cl	cider vinegar	2½ fl oz
	freshly ground black pepper		1	Batavian endive, trimmed, and cut into strips	1
1 tbsp	virgin olive oil	1 tbsp			
2	onions, thinly sliced	2	2	ripe tomatoes, cored and cut into thin wedges	2
2	garlic cloves, finely chopped	2	45 g	feta cheese	1½ oz
2 tsp	fresh thyme	2 tsp			

Preheat the oven to 180°C (350°F or Mark 4). Sprinkle the lamb with the salt and plenty of pepper; Place it in a heavy roasting pan and roast it until it is tender—1½ to 2 hours—turning it once after 1 hour and adding 2 or 3 tablespoons of water if the juices begin to burn. Remove from the oven and set it aside to cool; do not wash the roasting pan. When the meat is cool enough to handle, pull it off the bone and tear it into shreds. Transfer the meat to a bowl, cover it loosely with aluminium foil, and keep it warm.

Spoon off any fat that has accumulated in the roasting pan and set the pan over a low heat. Stir in the oil, onions, garlic, thyme, mustard and a generous grinding of pepper. Cook the mixture, scraping up the caramelized juices with a wooden spoon, until the onions are translucent—10 to 15 minutes. Pour in the vinegar and continue cooking the mixture, stirring constantly, for 1 minute. Add the endive and the tomato wedges, and keep stirring the salad until the endive begins to wilt—about 1 minute. Stir in the shredded lamb and toss well.

Transfer the tossed salad to a serving bowl. Then crumble the feta cheese on top and serve the salad while it is still warm.

Spinach and Lamb Strudel

Serves 4

Working time: about 30 minutes

Total time: about 1 hour and 15 minutes

Calories 200

Protein 23g

Cholesterol 70mg

Total fat 7g

Saturated fat 3g

Sodium 235mg

300 g	lean lamb, trimmed and finely diced	**10 oz**
250 g	fresh spinach, washed and stemmed	**8 oz**
250 g	button mushrooms, finely chopped	**8 oz**
1	onion, finely chopped	**1**
30 g	wholemeal breadcrumbs	**1 oz**

2	garlic cloves, crushed	**2**
¼ tsp	salt	**¼ tsp**
	freshly ground black pepper	
2	sheets phyllo pastry, each 45 by 30 cm (18 by 12 inches)	**2**
½ tsp	safflower oil	**½ tsp**
1 tsp	sesame seeds	**1 tsp**
	cherry tomatoes for garnish	

Preheat the oven to 190°C (375°F or Mark 5).

Set aside four spinach leaves for garnish then plunge the rest into boiling water, bring it back to the boil and cook for 1 minute. Drain it in a colander and rinse under cold water, then squeeze it dry and chop it finely.

Brush a non-stick frying pan with oil, heat it over a high heat then sear the lamb quickly. Remove the pan from the heat and stir in the spinach, mushrooms, onion, breadcrumbs, garlic, salt and pepper. Mix all the ingredients thoroughly together

Lay one sheet of the phyllo on a work surface and cover it with the second sheet.

Spoon the lamb filling along one short side of the phyllo, keeping it 2.5 cm (1 inch) away from the edge. Shape the filling into a firm sausage with your fingers. Roll up the strudel and transfer it to a baking sheet, seam side down. Squeeze the ends of the phyllo together lightly to stop the filling falling out. Brush the strudel with the oil and sprinkle it with the sesame seeds. Bake it until the pastry is golden—about 40 minutes. Leave it to cool for about 5 minutes before cutting it into eight slices. Serve the strudel garnished with the reserved spinach leaves and cherry tomatoes.

Sweet Pepper and Lamb Lasagne

Serves 6

Working time: about 45 minutes

Total time about 1 hour and 45 minutes

Calories 315

Protein 25g

Cholesterol 50mg

Total fat 10g

Saturated fat 4g

Sodium 290mg

350 g	lean lamb, minced	**12 oz**
1	onion, chopped	**1**
1	garlic clove, chopped	**1**
2	sticks celery, chopped	**2**
2 tbsp	tomato paste	**2 tbsp**
12.5 cl	red wine	**4 fl oz**
12.5 cl	unsalted brown stock	**4 fl oz**
1	bay leaf	**1**
½ tsp	salt	**½ tsp**
	freshly ground black pepper	
9	'no pre-cook' lasagne strips	**9**

30 g	margarine	**1 oz**
30 g	plain flour	**1 oz**
30 cl	skimmed milk	**½ pint**
30 g	Parmesan cheese, grated	**1 oz**
	white pepper	
	Sweet pepper sauce	
3	sweet peppers, sliced	**3**
30 cl	passata	**½ pint**
2	garlic cloves, crushed	**2**
1 tsp	each of thyme and oregano	**1 tsp**
½ tbsp	cornflour	**½ tbsp**

Heat a heavy sauté pan over medium heat and seal the lamb. Add the onion and continue stirring until soft. Add the garlic, celery, tomato paste, wine, stock and bay leaf; Season, cover and cook for 30 minutes.

Put the sweet peppers, passata, garlic, thyme and oregano into a heavy saucepan, cover and simmer for 15 minutes. Then blend the cornflour with tablespoons of water and stir it in until the sauce thickens. Set aside.

Preheat the oven to 190°C (375°F or Mark 5).

Arrange three strips of lasagne in the bottom of a baking dish. Spread on the sweet pepper sauce, then make a second layer of pasta. Cover with the lamb mixture and put the remaining strips of lasagne on top.

Melt the margarine in a saucepan, add the flour and stir for 1 minute, then gradually add the milk and cook for 3 minutes. Stir in half of the Parmesan and season with white pepper.

Pour the topping over the lasagne. Sprinkle it with Parmesan and bake for 40 to 45 minutes.

Burghul Layered with Lamb and Fruit

Serves 5

Working Time: about 30 minutes

Total Time: about 1 hour and 45 minutes

Calories 350

Protein 30g

Cholesterol 75mg

Total fat 13g

Saturated fat 4g

Sodium 335mg

600 g	thin lamb slices, trimmed and flattened into escalopes	**1¼ lb**
1 tsp	virgin olive oil	**1 tsp**
1	small onion, sliced	**1**
1 tsp	salt	**1 tsp**
	freshly ground black pepper	
90 g	dried apricots, thoroughly rinsed	**3 oz**
1 tsp	ground cinnamon	**1 tsp**
½ tsp	ground coriander	**½ tsp**
250 g	burghul	**8 oz**
2 tbsp	finely chopped mint	**2 tbsp**
60 g	raisins	**2 oz**
90 g	fresh dates, stoned and halved	**3 oz**

Heat the oil in a heavy frying pan until it is very hot. Quickly brown the lamb slices—about 30 seconds on each side—and transfer them to a fireproof casserole. Reduce the heat and cook the onion in the frying pan, stirring, for 2 to 3 minutes, until soft. Season the lamb slices with ½ teaspoon of the salt and a little pepper, then add the onion to the casserole, together with the apricots, cinnamon and coriander. Cover with boiling water and simmer for 1 hour or until tender.

Soak the burghul in twice its volume of cold water for 30 minutes. Strain off any resdual liquid, add the mint and the remaining ½ teaspoon of salt and stir well.

Add the raisins and halved dates to the casserole and allow them to warm through—2 to 3 minutes. Strain the stock from the casserole through a sieve into a saucepan. Boil it rapidly until only about 12.5 cl (4 fl oz) of liquid remains, then pour the reduced stock back on to the meat and fruit.

Layer the soaked burghul and the lamb mixture in a large casserole, beginning and ending with a layer of burghul. Place a four fold layer of muslin over the top of the and seal with foil. Put the casserole on a trivet inside a larger pot and pour boiling water into the outer pot to a depth of about 5 cm (2 inches). Cover the outer pot and steam gently for about 30 minutes. Serve the dish hot from the casserole.

Layered Lamb Bake with Fennel

Serves 6

Working time: about 45 minutes

Total time: about 1 hour and 30 minutes

Calories 350

Protein 29g

Cholesterol 75mg

Total fat 14g

Saturated fat 6g

Sodium 390mg

6	loin chops (about 150g/5 oz each), trimmed	6
850 g	potatoes, peeled and thinly sliced	1¾ lb
8 cl	skimmed milk	8 fl oz
400 g	courgettes, trimmed and thinly sliced	14 oz
850 g	bulb fennel, trimmed and thinly sliced, trimmings reserved	1¾ lb
½ tsp	salt	½ tsp
¼ tsp	ground nutmeg	¼ tsp
	freshly ground black pepper	
20 g	polyunsaturated margarine, melted	¾ oz
3 tsp	grated lemon rind	3 tsp
2 tsp	chopped bulb fennel tops	2 tsp
	lemon wedges, for garnish	
	sprigs of bulb fennel tops, for garnish.	

Preheat the oven to 220°C (425°F or Mark 7)

Rinse the potato slices in cold water and pat them dry. Pour half of the milk into a shallow ovenproof dish. Arrange one third of the potato slices over the base of the dish. Cover the potato slices with half of the courgettes, and top these with half of the fennel. Season with one third of the salt, half of the nutmeg and some pepper. Over the fennel, layer half of the remaining potatoes and then the remaining courgettes and fennel. Season as before and add the remaining milk. Top the dish with overlapping slices of potato, brush them evenly with the margarine and cover with foil. Bake in the oven for 30 minutes.

To prepare the chops, mix the remaining third of the salt, some pepper and the lemon rind. Rub some of this over the chops. Secure the chops into neat rounds with cocktail sticks. Chop the reserved fennel trimmings and stuff a teaspoon of the chopped fennel into the space between the flap and fillet of each chop.

Arrange the chops on top of the vegetables and return to the oven, uncovered, for 20 to 30 minutes. Remove the cocktail sticks. Serve garnished with lemon and fennel.

Baked Stuffed Onions

Serves 4

Working time:
about 30
minutes

Total time:
about 1 hour
and 10
minutes

Calories
215
Protein
25g
Cholesterol
75mg
Total fat
10g
Saturated fat
3g
Sodium
170mg

350 g	lean lamb, trimmed and minced	**12 oz**
4	large Spanish onions	**4**
	(about 250 g/8 oz each)	
125 g	celeriac, peeled and chopped	**4 oz**
60 g	button mushrooms, chopped	**2 oz**
1 tsp	chopped fresh marjoram	**1 tsp**

4 tbsp	grated horseradish	**4 tbsp**
30 g	cashew nuts, coarsely chopped	**1 oz**
¼ tsp	salt	**¼ tsp**
	freshly ground black pepper	
	celery leaves, for garnish	

Peel the onions, trimming off the root ends, but leaving the tops intact. Place them in a large saucepan of simmering water and cook them until they are soft but still keep their shape—about 10 minutes. Drain and cool. Slice lids off the pointed ends, about a quarter of the way down each onion. Push out the centres of the onions with a teaspoon, leaving shells about two layers thick. (Save the centres for a soup or stock.)

Preheat the oven to 180°C (350°F or Mark 4). Lightly brush a non-stick frying pan with oil and heat it over high heat. Add the lamb, stirring until it changes colour—about 2

minutes. Add the celeriac, mushrooms and marjoram, reduce the heat to medium, and cook for a further 2 minutes. Stir in the horseradish, cashew nuts, salt and some pepper and remove the pan from the heat.

Place the onion shells in a shallow ovenproof dish. Using a teaspoon, pack the lamb mixture as tightly as possible into the shells, piling it up above the shells if necessary. Place the lids beside the onions, cover the dish with aluminium foil and bake the onions until they are tender—about 40 minutes. Replace the lids and serve the onions garnished with celery leaves.

Aubergine Fans

Serves 4

Working time:
about 45
minutes

Total time:
about 3 hours

Calories
275
Protein
20g
Cholesterol
60mg
Total fat
14g
Saturated fat
6g
Sodium
350 mg

4	aubergines, stemmed washed and dried	4
4	garlic cloves, quartered lengthwise	4
4	beef tomatoes, sliced thickly	4
175 g	mozzarella cheese, sliced thinly freshly ground black pepper	6 oz
60 g	fresh wholemeal breadcrumbs	2 oz
1	small egg, beaten	1

1 tbsp	grated Parmesan cheese	1 tbsp
	Basil spread	
30 g	fresh basil leaves, very finely chopped	1 oz
1 tbsp	extra virgin olive oil	1 tbsp
60 g	thick Greek yogurt	2 oz
1 tbsp	grated Parmesan cheese	1 tbsp
$\frac{1}{2}$ tsp	dry mustard	$\frac{1}{2}$ tsp

Preheat the oven to 180°C (350°F or Mark 4).

Slice the aubergines lengthwise, making cuts about 1 cm ($\frac{1}{2}$ inch) apart and leaving the slices joined by 3 to 4 cm ($1\frac{3}{4}$ to $1\frac{1}{2}$ inches) at the stem end. With the tip of a sharp knife, make four small cuts into the unsliced stem end. Press a slice of garlic into each cut.

For the basil spread, combine the chopped basil with the oil. Add the yogurt, Parmesan and mustard. Divide among the aubergines, spreading a little over each cut surface.

Sprinkle the tomato and mozzarella with plenty of black pepper. Place a slice or two of each between the segments of aubergine.

Select a baking dish wide enough to take all four aubergines. Brush the base lightly with oil and sprinkle it with 1 to 2 teaspoons of the breadcrumbs. Paint a little beaten egg over each aubergine, then sprinkle on the remaining breadcrumbs, pressing them down lightly. Arrange the aubergines in the oiled baking dish, pressing down on the upper surface of each to fan out the slices. Sprinkle the grated Parmesan over the fans.

Cover with foil, and bake for 2 to $2\frac{1}{2}$ hours. Remove the foil, increase the oven temperature to the maximum and continue to cook for 10 to 15 minutes, until the topping is crisp.

Lamb and Orange Pilaff

Serves 4

Working time
about 30
minutes

Total time
about 1 hour
and 25
minutes

Calories
385
Protein
16g
Cholesterol
55mg
Total fat
8g
Saturated fat
3g
Sodium
205mg

350 g	lean lamb, trimmed and finely diced	**12 oz**
1 tsp	safflower oil	**1 tsp**
1	onion, chopped	**1**
1	large leek, trimmed, washed and sliced	**1**
200 g	long-grain brown rice	**7 oz**
45 cl	unsalted brown or chicken stock	**¾ pint**
1 tsp	chopped fresh rosemary, or ½ tsp dried rosemary	**1 tsp**
¼ tsp	salt	**¼ tsp**
	freshly ground black pepper	
1	orange, rind grated and flesh cut into segments	**1**
2	carrots, peeled	**2**
125 g	courgettes, trimmed	**4 oz**
30 g	raisins	**1 oz**

Preheat the oven to 180 C (350 F or Mark 4).

Heat the oil in a fireproof casserole over high heat. Add the lamb and sear it quickly on all sides. Stir in the onion, leek and rice and cook them for 1 minute. Add the stock, rosemary, salt, pepper and orange rind. Bring the mixture to the boil, then cover the casserole, transfer it to the oven and bake the pilaff until the rice is almost tender and the liquid virtually absorbed—about 40 minutes.

Using a potato peeler, shred the carrots and courgettes into long strips. Reserve a few carrot strips for garnish and stir the remainder into the lamb mixture along with the courgette strips and the raisins. Return the casserole to the oven and cook, covered, until the rice and carrots are tender—about 20 minutes. Stir in the orange segments and garnish with the reserved carrot ribbons just before serving.

Port Paupiettes

Serves 8

Working time:
about 1 hour

Total time:
about 2 hours

Calories
220

Protein
27g

Cholesterol
75mg

Total fat
8g

Saturated fat
4g

Sodium
215mg

8	lamb slices (about 90 g/3 oz each) cut from the fillet end of the leg, trimmed and flattened	8
250 g	lean lamb, minced	8 oz
125 g	canned tomatoes, drained and seeded	4 oz
2 tbsp	chopped fresh tarragon	2 tbsp
¼ tsp	freshly ground black pepper	¼ tsp

¼ tsp	salt	¼ tsp
1 tsp	virgin olive oil	1 tsp
15 cl	ruby port	¼ pint
30 cl	unsalted brown stock	½ pint
6	black peppercorns	6
6	garlic cloves, unpeeled	6
1 tsp	arrowroot	1 tsp
2 tbsp	tomato paste	2 tbsp

Mix the minced lamb with the tomatoes, tarragon, black pepper and ½ teaspoon of the salt. Distribute among the slices of lamb and roll up each slice to form a paupiette. Secure in three or four places with string.

Preheat the oven to 170°C (325°F or Mark 3). Heat the oil in a large frying pan over medium heat. Sear the paupiettes, turning until evenly browned. Remove from the pan and place in a shallow casserole.

Increase the heat under the pan to high and pour in half the port. Bring to the boil and allow to bubble for a minute. Add the stock to the port and bring to the boil. Pour over the paupiettes. Add the peppercorns and garlic, cover and cook in the oven until the lamb is tender when pierced—about 1 hour. Remove the string and slice each paupiette into five. Arrange on a serving dish and keep warm.

Strain the stock into a saucepan. Discard the garlic and peppercorns. Add the remaining port and boil until it is reduced by one third and slightly syrupy. Mix the arrowroot with 1 tablespoon of water and add it to the sauce. Boil until the sauce clears. Add the remaining ¼ teaspoon of salt, remove from the heat and stir in the tomato paste. Serve the paupiettes with the hot sauce.

Phyllo-Wrapped Lamb Medallions

Serves 4

Working time: about 25 minutes

Total time: about 45 minutes

Calories 325
Protein 28g
Cholesterol 80mg
Total fat 12g
Saturated fat 4g
Sodium 320mg

1 kg	loin, boned and trimmed, eye only	**2¼ lb**	**12.5 cl**	port	**4 fl oz**
1	ripe pear	**1**	**1 tsp**	red wine vinegar	**1 tsp**
2 tsp	safflower oil	**2 tsp**	**12.5 cl**	unsalted brown stock	**4 fl oz**
¼ tsp	salt	**¼ tsp**	**4**	sheets phyllo pastry, each about 30 cm (12 inches) square	**4**
	freshly ground black pepper		**1**	egg white, lightly beaten	**1**
2 tsp	chopped fresh ginger root	**2 tsp**	**4**	parsley sprigs, for garnish (optional)	**4**

Peel, halve and core the pear, then thinly slice and set aside.

Slice the eye of loin into four equal pieces. Pound the pieces to a thickness of about 1 cm (½ inch). Heat the oil in a heavy frying pan over medium-high heat. Add the lamb medallions and sear for 1 minute on each side. Remove from the pan and season them with half the salt and some pepper; set aside.

Add the ginger, port, vinegar and chopped pear to the pan. Simmer the liquid until it is reduced by half—about 7 minutes. Add the stock, the remaining salt and some pepper and return to a simmer. Transfer the sauce to a blender, and purée it. Keep the sauce warm.

Preheat the oven to 220°C (425°F or Mark 7). Fold one of the phyllo sheets in half, keeping the others covered with a damp cloth. Pat a lamb medallion dry and position in the centre of the folded sheet. Arrange one quarter of the pear slices on top, then fold the phyllo over. Brush the seams with some of the beaten egg white. Put the phyllo package seam side down on a baking sheet. Brush the top with more egg white. Wrap the remaining lamb medallions in the same way.

Bake the packages for 8 minutes. Divide the sauce among four individual plates and set a phyllo package on each plate. Garnish with a sprig of parsley.

Lamb Tikka

Serves 4

Working time: about 30 minutes

Total time: about 5 hours (includes marinating)

Calories 255
Protein 32g
Cholesterol 75mg
Total fat 9g
Saturated fat 4g
Sodium 100mg

500 g	lean lamb, trimmed and cubed	**1 lb**
2.5 cm	fresh ginger root, coarsely chopped	**1 inch**
2	garlic cloves, coarsely chopped	**2**
2	green chili peppers, seeded and coarsely chopped	**2**
2 tsp	cumin seeds	**2 tsp**
1 tsp	ground turmeric	**1 tsp**
½ tsp	ground fenugreek	**½ tsp**
12	mint leaves	**12**
15 cl	plain low-fat yogurt	**¼ pint**
1 tbsp	fresh lime juice	**1 tbsp**
2	star anise pods	**2**
350 g	fresh pineapple, cut into chunks	**12 oz**

Put the meat in a bowl. In a blender or food processor, purée the ginger, garlic, chilies, cumin, turmeric, fenugreek and mint leaves. Add the yogurt and lime juice and blend to mix. Pour the purée over the meat, add the star anise and mix well to coat the meat. Leave the lamb to marinate in a cool place for 4 to 6 hours, stirring occasionally.

Preheat the grill. Thread the cubes of meat and pineapple alternately on to four metal kebab skewers; reserve the marinade. Place the kebabs on a grill rack and grill until the lamb is cooked but still slightly pink in the centre—10 to 15 minutes. Turn the skewers frequently and baste the meat with the reserved marinade while grilling. Serve hot.

Red Pepper and Okra Lamb Stew

Serves 4

Working time: about 20 minutes

Total time: about 1 hour

Calories
380
Protein
35g
Cholesterol
90mg
Total fat
13g
Saturated fat
4g
Sodium
125mg

600 g	lean lamb (from the leg or loin), trimmed of fat and cut into 2.5 cm (1 inch) pieces	**1¼ lb**
2 tbsp	plain flour	**2 tbsp**
2 tbsp	paprika	**2 tbsp**
⅛ tsp	salt	**⅛ tsp**
	freshly ground black pepper	
1 tbsp	safflower oil	**1 tbsp**
1	onion, finely chopped	**1**
2 tsp	cider vinegar	**2 tsp**
35 cl	unsalted brown or chicken stock	**12 fl oz**
1 tsp	Dijon mustard	**1 tsp**
8 drops	Tabasco sauce	**8 drops**
1	garlic clove, finely chopped	**1**
1	sweet red pepper, seeded, and cut into 2.5 cm (1 inch) strips	**1**
250 g	okra, trimmed, sliced diagonally into 2 cm (¾ inch) pieces	**8 oz**

Combine the flour and paprika in a large bowl. Season the lamb pieces with the salt and some freshly ground black pepper, then toss them in the flour mixture. Remove the meat from the bowl, shaking off any excess flour, and set it aside.

Heat 2 teaspoons of the oil in a fireproof casserole over medium-high heat. Add the lamb pieces and chopped onion, and cook them, stirring continuously, until the onion is translucent and the meat is browned—2 to 3 minutes. Stir in the stock, cider vinegar, mustard, Tasbaco sauce and chopped garlic, and bring the mixture to a simmer. Continue to simmer the stew for 30 minutes.

Heat the remaining teaspoon of oil in a non-stick frying pan over medium-high heat and stir-fry the sweet pepper strips and the sliced okra for 2 minutes. Then transfer the vegetables to the casserole containing the lamb and simmer the stew until the meat is tender—20 to 30 minutes.

Lamb Sausages on Skewers

Serves 4

Working time:
about 30
minutes

Total time:
about 1 hour
and 10
minutes

Calories
245
Protein
26g
Cholesterol
75mg
Total fat
11g
Saturated fat
4g
Sodium
320mg

600 g	lean lamb, trimmed and minced	**1¼ lb**
1	large ripe tomato, chopped	**1**
¼ tsp	salt	**¼ tsp**
	freshly ground black pepper	
1 tsp	sugar	**1 tsp**
1 tbsp	red wine vinegar	**1 tbsp**
3 tbsp	chopped parsley	**3 tbsp**

1 tbsp	chopped fresh oregano	**1 tbsp**
1 tbsp	virgin olive oil	**1 tbsp**
30 g	dry breadcrumbs	**1 oz**
2	spring onions, trimmed and thinly sliced	**2**
½ tsp	capers, rinsed	**½ tsp**
12.5 cl	plain low-fat yogurt	**4 fl oz**

Put the tomato, half of the salt, some pepper, the sugar and the vinegar into a heavy frying pan set over medium heat. Cook, stirring frequently, until only 4 tablespoons remain—about 20 minutes. Transfer the mixture to a bowl and let it cool to room temperature.

Combine the lamb with 2 tablespoons of the parsley, the oregano, egg white, half of the oil, the breadcrumbs, half of the spring onions, the remaining salt and some pepper. Stir the cooled tomato mixture into the lamb mixture and refrigerate the bowl until the contents are thoroughly chilled—about 30 minutes.

Preheat the grill for 10 minutes.

Divide the lamb mixture into four portions and form each one into a sausage shape about 10 cm (4 inches) long. Thread each sausage on to a skewer, keeping the meat pressed firmly in place.

Lightly coat the sausages by rolling them in the remaining oil. Grill the sausages, turning the skewers every now and then, until the meat is lightly browned—8 to 10 minutes.

Meanwhile, finely chop the remaining parsley with the remaining spring onions and the capers. Transfer the chopped parsley mixture to a small bowl and whisk in the yoghurt and some pepper. Serve the sausages immediately, passing the sauce separately.

Roast Shoulder with Rosemary

Serves 12

Working time: about 40 minutes

Total time: about 3 hours (includes marinating)

Calories 310

Protein 20g

Cholesterol 75mg

Total fat 12g

Saturated fat 5g

Sodium 130mg

2.5 kg	shoulder of lamb, trimmed	**3 lb**	
1 tbsp	virgin olive oil	**1 tbsp**	
2 tsp	mixed dried herbs	**2 tsp**	
½ tsp	salt	**½ tsp**	
4	long rosemary sprigs	**4**	
1½ tsp	plain flour	**1½ tsp**	
60 cl	unsalted chicken or brown stock	**1 pint**	
	freshly ground black pepper		

Make four diagonal incisions with a sharp knife across the shoulder, almost down to the bone. Rub the olive oil, mixed herbs and salt all over the lamb, then insert the rosemary sprigs in the diagonal cuts. Place the shoulder in a roasting pan and set it aside in a cool place to marinate for 1 hour. Preheat the oven to 220°C (425°F or Mark 7).

Roast the shoulder for 15 minutes, then reduce the oven temperature to 190°C (375°F or Mark 5) and roast the meat for a further 45 minutes to 1 hour for rare to medium meat, basting frequently with the pan juices. Transfer the shoulder of lamb to a serving dish, cover it loosely with foil and set it aside

in a warm place while you make the gravy.

Tip the roasting pan slightly so that the juices run to one corner, then skim off any fat. Sprinkle the flour over the juices left in the pan and stir well with a wooden spoon until the juices and flour are blended. Gradually add the stock, stirring continuously. Place the pan over moderate heat and bring the gravy to the boil, stirring all the time until it thickens; season with some black pepper. Reduce the heat to low and simmer for 6 to 8 minutes, stirring occasionally. Strain the gravy through a sieve into a warmed gravy boat and serve it with the roast shoulder.

Shoulder Stuffed with Wild Rice and Spinach

Serves 12

Working time:
about 1 hour

Total time:
about 4 hours

Calories
225

Protein
22g

Cholesterol
75mg

Total fat
13g

Saturated fat
5g

Sodium
140mg

1.5 kg	shoulder of lamb, boned	**3 lb**	**½ tsp**	finely grated nutmeg	**½ tsp**
60 g	wild rice	**2 oz**	**¼ tsp**	salt	**¼ tsp**
2 tsp	virgin olive oil	**2 tsp**		freshly ground black pepper	
4	shallots, coarsely chopped	**4**	**30 cl**	unsalted chicken stock	**½ pint**
175 g	celeriac, grated	**6 oz**	**1 tsp**	cornflour	**1 tsp**
175 g	fresh spinach, washed, stemmed	**6 oz**			

Wash the wild rice and put it into a large saucepan in twice its volume of water. Bring to the boil, cover the pan and simmer until the husks have split and the rice is soft—50 minutes to 1 hour. Drain the rice. Heat the oil in a frying pan, add the shallots and cook them until soft. Add the celeriac and cook until it begins to look transparent—about 3 minutes—then add the spinach and cook for about 1 minute, until it wilts. Blend this mixture very briefly in a food processor to make a rough-textured purée. Mix with the wild rice, and season with the nutmeg, ½ teaspoon salt and some black pepper.

Preheat the oven to 230°C (450°F or Mark 8). Stuff and tie the shoulder into a melon shape. Put the lamb in a roasting pan and season the outside with the remaining salt and some pepper. Roast the lamb in the oven until well browned—10 to 15 minutes—then reduce the oven temperature to 200°C (400°F or Mark 6) and cook for a further 1¼ to 1½ hours. Transfer to a carving board and allow it to rest in a warm place for 15 minutes.

Skim off any fat from the surface of the roasting juices and transfer the pan to the stove top. Add the stock and boil, stirring. Mix the cornflour with 1 tablespoon of water and add it to the pan, stirring constantly until the gravy thickens—2 to 3 minutes. Season with black pepper. Cut off the string and carve the lamb into wedges. Serve the gravy separately.

Roast Saddle of Lamb with Plum Sauce

Serves 12

Working time:
about 1 hour

Total time:
about 2 hours
and 40
minutes

Calories
335
Protein
28g
Cholesterol
75mg
Total fat
14g
Saturated fat
6g
Sodium
180mg

4.5 kg	saddle of lamb	**10 lb**
1 tbsp	virgin olive oil	**1 tbsp**
2 tbsp	demerara sugar	**2 tbsp**
¾ tsp	salt	**¾ tsp**
	freshly ground black pepper	
750 g	large purple plums, halved and stoned	**1½ lb**
60 cl	red wine	**1 pint**
2.5 cm	piece cinnamon stick	**1 inch**
15 cl	unsalted chicken stock	**¼ pint**

Preheat the oven to 220°C (425°F or Mark 7). Spread the saddle of lamb out flat on a cutting board and trim off the fatty strip, or apron, of flesh along each side; leave just enough to overlap slightly when tucked underneath. Trim any excess fat from the meat.

Rub the olive oil over the meat, then sprinkle with the sugar, ½ teaspoon of the salt and some black pepper. Tuck the side flaps underneath and place it in a roasting pan.

Roast the saddle for 20 minutes, then reduce the oven temperature to 180°C (350°F or Mark 4) and place the halved plum closely round the lamb. Pour half of the wine over the lamb and add the piece of cinnamon. Continue roasting for 1¼ to 1½ hours. Baste the meat frequently while it roasts; each time you baste, add some more of the wine until it is all used up.

When the lamb is cooked, transfer it to a large, hot serving platter. Cover, and allow it to rest in a warm place for about 20 minutes.

Meanwhile, make the plum sauce. Set a nylon sieve over a non-reactive saucepan and pour the juices from the roasting pan into it. Using a wooden spoon, press the halved plums through the sieve into the saucepan. Stir the chicken stock into the plum mixture and season it with the remaining salt and some black pepper. Heat the sauce through, then pour it into a warmed sauce boat.

This dish may be served with a garnish of glazed fruit, as illustrated.

Useful weights and measures

Weight Equivalents

Avoirdupois		*Metric*
1 ounce	=	28.35 grams
1 pound	=	254.6 grams
2.3 pounds	=	1 kilogram

Liquid Measurements

$^1/_4$ pint	=	$1^1/_2$ decilitres
$^1/_2$ pint	=	$^1/_4$ litre
scant 1 pint	=	$^1/_2$ litre
$1^3/_4$ pints	=	1 litre
1 gallon	=	4.5 litres

Liquid Measures

1 pint	= 20 fl oz	= 32 tablespoons
$^1/_2$ pint	= 10 fl oz	= 16 tablespoons
$^1/_4$ pint	= 5 fl oz	= 8 tablespoons
$^1/_8$ pint	= $2^1/_2$ fl oz	= 4 tablespoons
$^1/_{16}$ pint	= $1^1/_4$ fl oz	= 2 tablespoons

Solid Measures

1 oz almonds, ground = $3^3/_4$ level tablespoons

1 oz breadcrumbs fresh = 7 level tablespoons

1 oz butter, lard = 2 level tablespoons

1 oz cheese, grated = $3^1/_2$ level tablespoons

1 oz cocoa = $2^3/_4$ level tablespoons

1 oz desiccated coconut = $4^1/_2$ tablespoons

1 oz cornflour = $2^1/_2$ tablespoons

1 oz custard powder = $2^1/_2$ tablespoons

1 oz curry powder and spices = 5 tablespoons

1 oz flour = 2 level tablespoons

1 oz rice, uncooked = $1^1/_2$ tablespoons

1 oz sugar, caster and granulated = 2 tablespoons

1 oz icing sugar = $2^1/_2$ tablespoons

1 oz yeast, granulated = 1 level tablespoon

American Measures

16 fl oz	=1 American pint
8 fl oz	=1 American standard cup
0.50 fl oz	=1 American tablespoon

(slightly smaller than British Standards Institute tablespoon)

0.16 fl oz	=1 American teaspoon

Australian Cup Measures
(Using the 8-liquid-ounce cup measure)

1 cup flour	4 oz
1 cup sugar (crystal or caster)	8 oz
1 cup icing sugar (free from lumps)	5 oz
1 cup shortening (butter, margarine)	8 oz
1 cup brown sugar (lightly packed)	4 oz
1 cup soft breadcrumbs	2 oz
1 cup dry breadcrumbs	3 oz
1 cup rice (uncooked)	6 oz
1 cup rice (cooked)	5 oz
1 cup mixed fruit	4 oz
1 cup grated cheese	4 oz
1 cup nuts (chopped)	4 oz
1 cup coconut	$2^1/_2$ oz

Australian Spoon Measures

	level tablespoon
1 oz flour	2
1 oz sugar	$1^1/_2$
1 oz icing sugar	2
1 oz shortening	1
1 oz honey	1
1 oz gelatine	2
1 oz cocoa	3
1 oz cornflour	$2^1/_2$
1 oz custard powder	$2^1/_2$

Australian Liquid Measures
(Using 8-liquid-ounce cup)

1 cup liquid	8 oz
$2^1/_2$ cups liquid	20 oz (1 pint)
2 tablespoons liquid	1 oz
1 gill liquid	5 oz ($^1/_4$ pint)